How
Meditation
Heals

How
Meditation
Heals

A Scientific Explanation

Eric Harrison

Ulysses Press
Berkeley, California

Published by: Ulysses Press
P.O. Box 3440
Berkeley, CA 94703
www.ulyssespress.com

Library of Congress Catalog Card Number: 00-110580
ISBN: 1-56975-264-8

First published in 2000 by Judy Piatkus Publishers, Ltd.

Printed in Canada by Transcontinental Printing

10 9 8 7 6 5 4 3 2 1

Editorial and production staff: Leslie Henriques, Steven Zah Schwartz,
   Claire Chun, Demetra Markis, Lily Chou, Lisa Kester
Design: Sarah Levin
Cover Illustration: "Reddy #2," Diana Ong/SuperStock

Distributed in the United States by Publishers Group West

This book has been written and published strictly for informational purposes, and in no way should it be used as a substitute for consultation with your medical doctor or other health care professional. All facts in this book came from published trade books, self-published materials by experts, magazine articles, personal interviews, and the personal-practice experiences of the author or of authorities quoted or sources cited. You should not consider educational material herein to be the practice of medicine or to replace consultation with a physician or other medical practitioner. The author and publisher are providing you with information in this work so that you can have the knowledge and can choose, at your own risk, to act on that knowledge. The author and publisher also urge all readers to be aware of their health status and to consult health professionals before beginning any health program, including changes in dietary habits.

Contents

❋

Preface

❋

It is no mistake that the Buddha is usually shown with a faint smile on his face. Meditation is a delight—better than food or sex or a good night's sleep. It also feels good for our health, though most people would be hard pressed to say why.

In this book, I explain the links between health, relaxation and meditation. The argument goes as follows: Ill-health is a state of imbalance, or stress, within the various functions of the body. Relaxation is the process that helps restore equilibrium so the body can repair itself. Meditation is the art of consciously relaxing, which accelerates the process.

We could put this another way. Meditation settles the mind and relaxes the body. This restores a state of internal balance, or "homeostasis," which is the optimum state for self-repair and healing. By relaxing deeply when we can, and by staying relaxed during the day, the health benefits can be enormous.

The first four chapters of this book clarify the key concepts of health, relaxation and meditation. The chapters on meditation enable you to start practicing immediately if you want to. This overview is not as comprehensive as my other book, *Teach Yourself to Meditate,* but is quite enough to get you started. There are other meditations throughout the text, about 40 in all.

The rest of the book describes how meditation helps with common ailments. If you want, you can turn to the chapter that attracts you immediately, but you'll probably find most of them useful. The sequence of ailments runs from those that seem more physical to those that seem more mental.

In reality, pain is just as psychological an event as anxiety, but I start with the more "physical" ailments because they are easier to influence directly. For example, we can consciously relax tight facial muscles—they are within our direct control. But we have to use indirect methods such as meditation to lower the elevated levels of adrenaline that go with chronic anxiety, for example.

The Evidence

A meditation session affects our physiology in subtle but obvious ways. After a ten-minute meditation almost anyone should be able to say, "Yes, my muscles have relaxed, I am breathing more easily and my mind is less agitated." It follows that it could have more far-reaching benefits as well.

Personally I see the results of meditation every working day. Since 1987, I have run the Perth Meditation Centre in Western Australia. I have taught around 15,000 people to meditate, most of whom have attended at least one course of seven weeks duration. I have seen this unspectacular activity lead to huge improvements in physical and mental health. It can transform people in ways that any psychologist or physician would envy.

Many doctors and psychologists understand how a patient's state of mind affects his or her health, but they have to be cautious about recommending meditation as a treatment. There are many charlatans in the alternative health field, selling hope and placebos to sick people.

However, meditation itself has passed the test. There are now decades of substantial scientific research on meditation. We know that it helps with certain common ailments, and makes the body and mind function better in measurable ways. Many doctors realize that this can be enough to markedly improve a patient's health. About a quarter of my students are now referred to me by medical practitioners.

Although the connection between body and mind is self-evident, it is difficult to scientifically investigate. Psychologists evaluate mental states and scientists measure biological functions but there is no lingua franca between them. The units of measurement and methodologies used in these two disciplines are so different it is all but impossible to connect them.

We know, for example, that fear and anger (which are the province of psychology) activate the sympathetic nervous system (the province of medicine). We can measure the chemistry involved in exquisite detail, but how on earth do you measure fear or anger? Or even scientifically define the difference between them?

As a result, there is hardly any good scientific literature on the body/mind connection. What there is tends to be tentative and struggling to define its terms. However, there are a few fine books available, and at the end of this book I review the main texts I have used, if you want to research them.

Many doctors, nurses and medically trained people have read the earlier edition of this book. They have reassured me that my descriptions of physiological processes contain very few inaccuracies that would trouble a professional. With this in mind, I have kept the medical references and footnotes to a minimum, so the book reads smoothly for the layman.

Meditation as a Health Management Skill

In this book, I talk particularly about the illnesses and deteriorating conditions we are all prone to. Rather than addressing every ailment, I have tried to present the principles of meditation sufficiently clearly for the reader to adapt to his or her own situation. And while meditation can produce dramatic turnarounds in illness, it is even more valuable as a preventative measure.

Managing one's health is complicated. There is rarely a single cause to any illness. The body operates as an interlocking network of multiple functions. Staying healthy is not a matter of knocking out individual illnesses when they arise. It is more about paying attention to an array of small details on a daily basis and thereby slowing the rate of aging, or "wear and tear" in the body.

Who among us, apart from perhaps the very young, feels 100% healthy? We are all somewhere on a sliding scale between total health and total disability. In my case, I am a healthy fifty-year-old, and have rarely been sick enough to take a day off work. Nonetheless, my heart and lung function is not what it was thirty years ago. My digestive system is more choosy. There is probably more plaque build-up in the veins and traces of arthritis in the joints. I don't have heart disease or asthma or cancer, but I have the potential for all of them. I am already partly sick.

Meditation can help us maintain optimum function and delay the inevitable effects of aging. It helps us keep our blood pressure under control before it leads to a stroke. By sleeping better, we have more energy and our immune system is more efficient. We breathe better, manage pain better and digest food better. Meditation helps us manage our health intelligently before the damage becomes irreparable.

To someone considering meditation for health reasons, it can seem a strange activity and its health claims rather implausible. In this book, I try to bring the whole matter down to earth. Meditation is easy to do. It has clear physical results that you can see if you look for them. The medical evidence clearly shows how relaxation is essential for the healthy functioning of the body. Whether you are sick, or want to maintain your health, or simply want to enjoy life more, you will find that meditation is worth looking into.

Eric Harrison
Perth, Western Australia
March 2001

PART ONE

Explaining Meditation

❀

ONE

Health Is the Art of Balance

❀

Sickness is a state of imbalance. Conversely, health is a state of balance, when all the body's systems are functioning as they should. Since this simple but subtle idea runs through the whole book, I'll describe it in more detail now.

Our bodies are designed to cope with extremes. My heart rate could reach 180 beats per minute, or my temperature could go to 103 degrees, or I could be deprived of food, water or sleep temporarily without damage. But to remain healthy, I need to return to a more balanced state fairly quickly.

"Homeostasis" is the medical term for this state of internal balance. It assumes the body functions best at certain ideal levels of oxygen needs, blood acidity, available energy and so on, and ill-health results when these are pushed to extremes too often. Our bodies are always striving to maintain or restore homeostasis against all the stresses we subject them to.[1]

Medicine tries to helps this process. Doctors look for signs of imbalance or "pathology," in order to correct them. A blood test may say your iron levels are 14.7 units, or sugar levels are 6.2 units, but it will also say what the normal range should be. If you fall outside it, the doctor knows where to act.

Often the tests come back normal, but you still feel off-color. Perfect balance, or homeostasis, is found somewhere in the center of that "normal range," given your particular makeup. So we can describe pathology as being outside the normal range, middling health as being within it and homeostasis as the ideal point in the center.

Traditionally, the term homeostasis was used to describe the body in a resting state, since this is as still as the body ever gets. In this state, the body is burning just enough energy to stay alive; but it also happens to be the optimum state for self-healing and physical growth. The body puts away the groceries, tidies the house and does structural repairs when in a state of rest.

This definition of homeostasis is a little narrow, and it has been extended in recent years. For example, we obviously burn more energy walking than sleeping, but this doesn't mean we are in an unbalanced state. We actually need to be active to stay healthy.

The term "homeostasis" can be extended to describe the point of balance amid the shifting activities of the day. All kinds of functions—sugar levels, muscle tension, oxygen consumption, hormonal secretions—fluctuate naturally during the day, depending on the time and our activity. If these stay within sustainable limits, we can say we are in "allostatic balance."[2]

We can feel this as the difference between pacing ourselves well and stressing out, between leading a busy but satisfying life and lurching from crisis to crisis. Usually we are in allostatic balance when our energy expenditure is appropriate to the situation we're in.

Homeostasis usually refers to the body in a state of rest, but it also includes the concept of "allostasis"—being in balance while active. These two terms conveniently relate to the two ways we think of "relaxation": i.e., as deep rest, and as a state of enjoyable activity. In this book, I will use the word "balance" to refer to either state.

Health Is a Balancing Act

Did you ever try to balance on a seesaw in a kid's playground? A seesaw is just a plank on a fulcrum, but if you stand above the center

point you can keep both ends of the plank off the ground. You undoubt-
edly found out that balance is not a fixed point of stillness. You just
can't stand still on a seesaw. You have to wobble.

You would also find that little wobbles were easily corrected. If
you could keep your wobbles small, you could stay there a long time.
However, a big swing left would need a desperate lurch to the right to
keep the plank from crashing.

Our bodies work the same way. Small oscillations are natural and
manageable. For example, we oscillate between activity and inactivity
every day. But when activity becomes hyperactivity, we go beyond the
point of allostatic balance and feel stressed. You can see how the old
maxim of "moderation in all things" relates to the body.

Small oscillations are inevitable, but even the occasional big swing
is quite healthy and even good for us. Our bodies are designed to cope
with maximum stresses for short periods, and they benefit from the
practice. This is why a few bursts of aerobic exercise each week are so
valuable. They keep the veins and arteries supple and ventilate the
lungs, even though the body is temporarily pushed beyond the point
of sustainable balance.

Similarly, our digestive systems should be able to process a huge
drunken meal within a few hours. Our heart should be able to race
from 70 to 170 beats a minute, if we are being chased by thugs. We
should be able to help a friend shift a refrigerator. Even exposure to a
flu virus can strengthen the immune system, and so on.

But if we are constantly overeating, being chased by thugs, attacked
by germs and moving refrigerators, we are in trouble. The principle is
that extreme stress is okay, so long as it is for a short time and we have
time to recover, but chronic stress is deadly. It could be argued that most
health problems come not from the stress, but from inadequate recov-
ery time—we don't relax deeply or long enough to repair ourselves.

Helping the Body Heal Itself

Our bodies do their utmost to maintain balance—after all, they will
die if they don't. The way they keep an eye on all those seesaws is quite

simple. A receptor will pick up a sign of imbalance and tell a control center, which usually inhibits what is creating the problem. This is called negative feedback, like a thermostat switching off a heater. For example, if lactic acid accumulates in an overworked muscle, the pain signals get the brain to stop the exertion until the muscle can recover.

We are mostly unconscious of the body's ongoing efforts to maintain allostatic balance. Within our bodies, the housecleaning, growth, repair and defense is done by squadrons of invisible servants who do the work much more intelligently than our egos ever could.

But when we get sick, our conscious mind gets in on the act. We ask, "What have I done? What can I do?" and we try to help the body's healing mechanisms. If we go to a doctor, he or she will also try to support or amplify what the body is already doing.

So if we feel exhausted, we try to restore balance by having a long sleep—just what the body would want, if you asked it. If you have severe pain, a doctor may reinforce the body's natural painkillers by giving you morphine. Even surgery to remove a tumor is just a gross way of doing the work of the T-cells and macrophages (the killers and scavengers in the bloodstream).

The seesaw principle of balance is simple, but our bodies are exquisitely complex. They contain eleven different biological systems, all interconnected and in constant flux. They are all monitored right down to the molecular level and kept in balance by the endocrine and nervous systems.

Some of these homeostatic systems are so tiny and sensitive they correct their imbalances within micro-seconds. Others take minutes and hours, while some psychological processes can take weeks and years. If your arm starts to ache while you're sawing wood, you'll stop within seconds. If you feel thirsty or hungry, you'll eat or drink something within minutes. If you're feeling exhausted from overwork, you'll probably wait 'til the evening or the weekend before you collapse.

You could imagine homeostasis as a network of thousands of oscillating seesaws within us, with several Big Daddy seesaws running the show. This means we don't have to make thousands of adjustments to bring ourselves back to balance. If we can get the main things right, there will be a ripple-down effect right through the body.

For example, we have some conscious control over our muscles and breathing. If we deliberately relax the facial muscles and let the breathing soften, this will indirectly affect blood pressure, hormone levels, digestive activity and so on.

Why Do We Get Sick?

Our bodies are extremely good at maintaining balance, so why do we still get sick? There are some causes that are largely beyond our control. The ravages of age or severe outer stressors such as war or starvation will wear us down, no matter what we do.

In theory, we could pace ourselves well and be in a balanced state all day long—eating, working, exercising and resting well. If we kept this going all our lives, there is a good chance we would live to a hale and hearty old age.

But, being conscious animals, we frequently ignore the signs of stress and overrule the intelligence of our bodies. We get overexcited and push ourselves to the limits. We eat and drink and work too much and eventually lose all concept of a balanced life. And though we often grind to a halt out of exhaustion, we usually don't let ourselves fully recover before plunging back into the fray.

We can also be mildly stressed for years at a time. To be 10% more stressed than you need to be can make you just as prone to middle-aged illness as extreme stress. Because mild continual stress is so common, we often take it as being "normal," and don't realize how insidious it is.

Many people are ill because they look for purely physical solutions to their health. In many ways, the more specific the medical intervention, the less it contributes to total health, and vice versa. If you take pills for high blood pressure, they are unlikely to improve your insomnia or indigestion or chronic pain. So you need to take pills for each of those, and maybe some antidepressants as well.

However, if you meditate to lower your blood pressure, the effect is less direct but can have wider benefits. Your hypertension improves but you also have less abdominal gas, you sleep better and your pain bothers you less. Meditation is less precise in effect than a diuretic, but it goes one step further back to a more fundamental cause: our over-active anxious minds.

Levels of Balance

The idea of health as a state of balance can be seen in many different ways. At one level, homeostasis refers to the ideal levels of things like blood sugar and acidity, digestive juices, hormones, kidney function and so on. We can't sense most of these, and they are beyond our direct control.

Going up the scale, balance refers to things we can sense and partially control such as muscle tension, hunger, thirst and fatigue. In particular, it relates to our sense of being relaxed or stressed at any time.

In a formal meditation, we may tune into the feeling of homeostasis as deep conscious relaxation. This feels so harmonious and emotionally nourishing, it is easy to see why it is an optimum state for health and self-repair. You only need to compare it with the tension that often precedes it to recognize how good it feels.

Gradually we can extend this sense of inner harmony amid the ordinary events of the day. We maintain this "allostatic" balance by pacing ourselves, conserving energy, reacting appropriately to things but not overreacting, and winding down quickly whenever we get the chance.

Eventually we notice how emotions affect our state of balance. There is no doubt that anxiety, irritability, depression, and a need for stimulation or excitement destabilize us. Conversely, other mind states feel harmonious. Contentment, peace, sensual pleasure and intellectual delight are all good predictors of health and long life.

Finally, the idea of health as balance has an existential dimension. I meet very few people who are contented cabbages. A healthy mind is inherently curious. It wants to know things: "Where am I going? What am I doing here?" If there are absolute truths, our minds won't rest until they find them. In this sense, "balance" relates to the psyche becoming mature and whole with the passing of the years.

Perhaps the best foundation for health and long life is to be profoundly content or happy, and there aren't any simple recipes for this. For most of us, a balanced and harmonious life usually requires decades of trial-and-error and a high degree of self-awareness.

Fortunately, we don't have to get everything right all at once. The meditation tradition is very clear in that you start right where you are. You just do what you can in the moment, rather than trying to plan the perfect life.

❋

TWO

The Biology of Relaxation

❋

This book is based on the idea that relaxation restores the body to a state of balance and health, and meditation augments this process. In this chapter, I explain how the tension-relaxation cycle works.

Our bodies and the systems within them naturally oscillate between activity and inactivity. A moderate oscillation is healthy, but big oscillations can lead to pathology. The extremes of stress and hyper-arousal are usually "balanced" by the extremes of exhaustion and sickness. In time, this disequilibrium accelerates the rate of wear and tear, and makes us vulnerable to illness and premature aging.

After something has stressed you out, your body's "relaxation response" tries to restore you to a state of balance. Unfortunately, this rarely works as smoothly as it should. If we overreact, we remain aroused for longer than necessary.

For example, if someone honks a car horn at us in anger, we can feel our bodies tense and our breath freeze. Once we realize we are overreacting, it's easy to laugh at ourselves and start breathing again.

But if we continue to think about the incident long after it has passed, its effect can linger. It may take us minutes or even hours to settle down. Even when we do relax, the progression can be erratic and incomplete. In fact, some people are incapable of being relaxed at all while awake. And though we all go to sleep sooner or later, that rest can be seriously compromised by the day's preoccupations.

We can be over-aroused even while doing the simplest of things. If you ask yourself while driving or cooking or shopping, "Am I tense or relaxed right now?" you will often realize you are out of balance. Paradoxically, this realization is usually enough to start you relaxing.

It seems such a small thing, to be a little tense while driving or cooking. However, it could be the main cause of our stress-related health problems. A chronic low level of tension can eat at us all day. If we are just 10% more aroused than we need to be, year after year, our health is bound to suffer.

The Autonomic Nervous System

The role of maintaining balance falls mainly on our autonomic nervous system. This operates something like a thermostat, oscillating between the two poles of arousal and relaxation. To mediate these changes, the nervous system is divided into two opposing "branches," each with a wide range of functions. In brief, we can say that the sympathetic branch of the nervous system winds us up and the parasympathetic branch winds us down.[1]

The term "relaxation response" describes the winding-down process. This expression was coined by respected researcher and writer Herbert Benson of the Harvard Medical School. The "relaxation response" is a shorthand way of saying, "the activity of the parasympathetic nervous system and the attendant hormonal processes."

In the "up," or arousal, phase, initiated by the sympathetic system, we feel anxious or excited. Adrenaline and noradrenaline are the main instigators. Our muscles tighten, blood pressure and breathing rates rise, and we burn a lot of energy fast. This often feels good, if it doesn't last too long. We can call this "the stress response."

In the "down" phase, governed by the parasympathetic system, the reverse happens. Adrenaline and noradrenaline levels fade, muscles relax, blood pressure and breathing rate drop, and we burn less energy as our metabolic rate slows down.

Within the one big daily cycle of being fully awake and fully asleep, there are many epicycles of partial arousal and partial relaxation. Left to itself, the body will naturally relax when tired and arouse itself after rest. Homeostasis is usually a state in which we are gently winding down or gently winding up.

The Physiology of Rapid Arousal

We can see what goes wrong if we look at states of extreme tension. Our bodies are hot-wired for rapid response to danger, real or imagined. If a grizzly bear lumbered into your room now, the sympathetic branch of your nervous system would respond within milliseconds. The purpose of this is to flood your body with energy to either fight or run away.

The hypothalamus tells the pituitary to tell the adrenal glands to produce adrenaline, and to release glucocorticoids into the bloodstream. At the same time, the other sympathetic nerves in the body will secrete noradrenaline, to amplify the effect.

The three big players in the stress response—adrenaline, noradrenaline and glucocorticoids—are reinforced by the activity of many smaller players. Vasopressin constricts blood vessels; endorphins and enkephalins suppress pain perception; thyroxine increases the metabolic rate, and so on.

Adrenaline and glucocorticoids cause the liver to release more glucose into the bloodstream. To circulate this energy around the body, adrenaline also speeds up the heart and breathing rates. This results in more fuel being available to the cells, increasing our body temperature and metabolic rate.

The immediate effects can be quite dramatic—they can even cause a heart attack! In a crisis, the heart can be pumping at up to five times its usual rate. The tiny circular muscles around the arteries contract, to help squirt the blood through quickly, and of course all the big muscles contract as well.

We recognize this feeling as "the adrenaline rush" (although thyroxine is probably more to blame). As the metabolic activity increases in the cells, a person feels agitated and shaky. His heart races, his breathing becomes rapid, and after a burst of energy, he tires easily.

The body acts like a nation at war, diverting resources from less important services to the battlefront. In effect, it conserves energy by shutting down those internal processes that can safely be postponed for a while. It shifts blood from the skin and the digestive system to the big muscles that govern movement. The immune system is inhibited, and the processes of energy storage and reproduction are switched off.

Chronic or Sustained Stress

All of this is perfectly appropriate if the crisis passes quickly. But if you stay this stressed, when do you start digesting your food again? And for how long can the heart and vascular system cope at this elevated rate? No one can remain at peak arousal for more than a few minutes without collapsing under the strain. Generally, the immediate response is modified fairly rapidly.

The initial stress response is triggered by what we can call our "emotional brain" (the limbic system). This tends to be rather blind, instinctive and extreme. Within a few seconds, however, our "thinking brain," the neo-cortex, comes into play. It more clearly assesses the situation and adds its input. Ideally, we experience a rapid arousal followed by a cooler appraisal and a return to equilibrium once the crisis has passed. This process is vividly described by Daniel Goleman in his book *Emotional Intelligence*.[2]

The physiological effects will thus be moderated depending on how the thinking mind interprets the problem. Thanks to our sophisticated neo-cortex, we now have hundreds of different possible responses. It is rare for us to go into a full fight-or-flight response, on any day. We have other options when we face a threat: we can argue, placate, threaten, reason, lie, abase ourselves . . . .

Each response is mediated by a different cocktail of hormones and nervous system activity. For example, adrenaline, sometimes called the "anger" hormone, is common in the classic fight-or-flight situation. Its close cousin noradrenaline, the "fear" hormone, and thyroxine are more common in the war of attrition that goes with chronic anxiety. Glucocorticoids are commonly implicated in states of depression.

The fight-or-flight response in itself, though definitely stressful, is not regarded as a health problem. A quick arousal and relatively quick return to allostatic balance is what animals commonly experience. Because they usually don't suffer chronic unresolved tension, they rarely have stress-related illnesses. Hence the title of one of my reference books: *Why Zebras Don't Get Ulcers*.

The Stress Response Can Be Enjoyable

Few of us go into full fight-or-flight response each day. More commonly, we face a string of smaller stressors that keep us in a state of quasi-arousal for hours or days at a time. This can be quite useful, and its bad effects minimized, if we pace ourselves and relax adequately.

The stress response acts on the body like a shot of strong coffee. Half an hour later we feel energized, with a zing in the body and a sparkling mind. The world seems to glow and we enjoy the challenges rather than shrinking from them. It is good to remember that the stress response is also triggered by positive excitement and pleasure.

If you ride this tiger well, you can be very productive. Coffee and/ or the sympathetic nervous system activity get many people going in the morning, and keep them on top of things during the day. Mild stress and excitement make the world go round. I personally find coffee helps my golf!

It is all a question of moderation and intelligent planning. You know that three hours after the coffee or the "adrenaline rush," you're likely to feel tired and mentally agitated if you don't do something. That increased metabolic activity burns out your fuel reserves, and you need to replenish them.

The Effects of Chronic Stress

The nervous and endocrine systems work well to keep our bodies in balance. Resilient as they are, abuse will eventually wear them down.

It's not hard to understand that the arousal symptoms described above, if sustained for too long, will be destructive.

High blood pressure leads to heart disease and kidney and respiratory failure. High metabolic rates lead to fatigue and cell damage. Muscular tension leads to physical pain and injury.

Constricted respiration combined with poor heart function contributes to asthma and to the kind of lung infections that commonly carry away the elderly.[3] Reduced blood supply to the digestive system, and excess production of hydrochloric acid in the stomach, produce a range of gastrointestinal problems.

The immune system, which protects the body from infection and disease, seems to suffer particularly under the pressure of chronic stress. Hans Seyle, the pioneer of bodymind science, discovered that the thymus gland, which is essential for the development of T-cells, will atrophy under stress. The lymphatic system (where pathogens are destroyed) and the spleen shrink.

The adrenal glands, like the heart, become enlarged when under constant pressure, and the white blood cell count drops. Decreased immunity makes one more susceptible to colds and the herpes virus,[4] and probably to more serious diseases as well.

A poor immune system affects everything. Many diseases such as arthritis, asthma, allergies and cancer seem particularly related to malfunctioning of the immune system. It is not surprising that stressed people succumb to illnesses that healthy people shrug off lightly. Years of inner warfare have destroyed their defense forces.

Will we get sick today, next week or next year? We all tend to have our own weak links that eventually give way under pressure. For example, we may be genetically prone to hypertension, gastrointestinal problems, arthritis or cancer. Our habitual stress levels may determine when, if ever, we succumb to our latent weakness.

Activating the Relaxation Response

Benson argues that with a little practice, we can learn to consciously activate the relaxation response. If stress is a factor in your illness, this is something you can do to help immediately. If your body is in a state of arousal, you can ameliorate that within minutes.

Once we talk about consciously relaxing, we are talking meditation. We can define meditation as any technique that consciously relaxes the body and settles the mind. Meditation invariably starts with conscious relaxation, though it obviously goes beyond this as well.

In general, meditation will activate the relaxation response where and when you need it. You could also say it reduces your metabolic rate when you are running too hot. It helps restore homeostasis after arousal. When you meditate, the body is back in self-repair and growth mode.

It also has a prophylactic effect. The psychophysiologist John Hoffman, at Harvard Medical School, found that "in people who regularly elicit the relaxation response, the body is less responsive to the hormone noradrenaline, even at those times when they are not specifically practicing the response." In other words, it resembles the alpha- and beta-blocker drugs that are commonly used to treat stress-related symptoms.[5]

Herbert Benson has shown that meditation has obvious physiological effects—a steep drop in metabolic activity, reduced blood lactate levels and muscle tension, slower breathing, drops in blood pressure for those whose pressure was high, a shift from the faster beta brain waves to the slower alpha, theta and delta waves, and subjective perceptions of relaxation and peace. In other words, meditation mirrored the effect of the relaxation response.[6]

He also found that meditation, as a conscious activity, does this faster and better than normal relaxation. Within a few minutes, meditators can commonly reduce their metabolic rate to a level that normally takes five hours of sleep to attain. As Benson notes, this means that meditation, though similar to sleep, is significantly different as well.

Such studies reinforce what meditators commonly feel: that meditation works faster and more efficiently than less structured forms of relaxation. People commonly say they find a few minutes meditation is better than an hour's sleep. Meditators often say sleep makes them dull, while meditation refreshes the mind. Or as Benson puts it, "After eliciting the relaxation response, the mind is more receptive to new information."[7]

Reading the Physiological Signs of Relaxation

At the very least, we can say meditation is good for our health because it relaxes the body. This hardly needs proof—you don't need experiments to prove that water is wet. By definition, meditation is a practice that relaxes the body. More convincing than any studies, however, is the personal confirmation people get when they meditate.

People who are reasonably sensitive to their bodies will notice at least some of the following signs of the relaxation response when they meditate: reduced muscular tension (e.g., the shoulders drop); reduced breath rate (indicating a slower metabolic rate); warmth or tingling on the skin (as the blood returns to the periphery); more saliva or activity in the digestive system (as it comes to life again); and more awareness of aches and pains (as the analgesic effect of the stress hormones wears off).

And of course, sleepiness. Usually at least one out of every four or five meditations you do is a little sleepier than you would like. Meditation usually involves slowing down to the border of sleep and wakefulness, and you invariably tip over the edge occasionally, if only for a few seconds at a time.

This is why good meditators rarely meditate lying down—they would lose it completely. You only have to look at any group of people meditating and notice the occasional bobbing head to know that meditation definitely activates the relaxation response.

Defusing the Mental Tension

When we first get sick, we naturally tend to think of health in physical terms, and regard relaxation as a way of relieving physical stress. In time, however, we realize that the causes of stress are emotional: they are in the way we respond to the world around us. Persistent irritability (i.e., anger) or anxiety (i.e., fear) can make us just as sick as an infection or a disease.

If stress were purely physical, we could fall asleep and all the tension of our lives would vanish. This is clearly never the case. Even in the happiest of lives we carry residual pain, tension, anxiety, disappointments, fears of the future and unresolved traumas from the past.

If we look at ourselves honestly, we notice how our typical behavior often undermines our well-being. We may be habitually manic or argumentative or complaining. We may try to please everyone or be a perfectionist or push ourselves beyond reasonable limits. These character traits can make us successful or well-liked, but they may also be ruining our health.

Although we long for the simple answer or formula that would solve all our problems, we rarely find it. Bookshops are full of such nostrums: follow this diet, join this group, purge the traumas of the past, embrace God, believe in yourself and so on. They all fall short because they don't treat us as individuals.

It seems that the only reliable approach is to listen to the ever-changing demands of our own body and mind. Our fundamental problem may be quite simple: we don't listen to ourselves very well. Some of us don't listen at all.

By meditating, we put the mental noise aside and create space to listen. For perhaps the first time in years we actually notice what our bodies feel like, and we see our habitual emotions clearly. Meditation doesn't give the answers as such. But when we see how much of our distress is caused by overreacting to circumstances, at least we know what to do. It's time to get serious about relaxation.

THREE

Meditation: The Basic Principles

Our minds have to work overtime to cope with our busy lives. Not surprisingly, the incessant mental activity often overwhelms us. Fatigue, stress, agitation, depression, mental confusion and ill-health are common outcomes.

Meditation doesn't work with the outer causes of stress. It simply cleans up the inner turmoil. Its approach is one of radical simplicity, and quite the opposite of our usual strategies: you just sit still and do nothing. Or "just watch" the inner dialogues without reacting.

It might sound easy, but have you ever tried it? The mind is very reluctant to do nothing at all. Even a calm mind is naturally mercurial and expansive. We seem to be genetically programmed to be curious. So in lieu of doing nothing (which is impossible), you do something as simple and stress-free as possible.

In other words, you focus. To keep the mind out of trouble, you focus on something simple (like the breath), or something pleasant (such as music). The mind will often take detours from the object, but even intermittent focus is enough to trigger the relaxation response. The object acts as an anchor, slowing the mind down.

While doing this, you are also learning to detach from thoughts. If a troublesome thought grabs you, you gradually pull free of it and return to the breath. As you relax, it is easier to "just watch," or be passively aware of, thoughts and sensations without needing to process them.

Focus, detachment, a passive awareness—these are the core skills in meditation. They all simplify the mental activity and conserve energy. Focusing on one thing is much simpler than racing from thought to thought. A passive awareness of thoughts and sensations is much simpler than actively engaging with them. And when you detach from a thought, there is a feeling of lightness and freedom.

If we do something simple, the body relaxes and the mind goes "Aaaahhhh." It is like reverting to a more elementary state of consciousness—a state of being, not doing. I find that children understand it perfectly well. Its simplicity makes it both effective and difficult. As sophisticated adults, used to thinking of a dozen things at once, we often find it hard to believe that doing virtually nothing has such far-reaching effects.

There are at least three reasons why it does. First, focusing on one thing is usually a pleasant escape from random thought. Second, it takes us into the present moment. Third, we are passively aware, rather than actively thinking. Let us look at these in more detail.

How Can We Escape Thinking?

Most of us think too much. The inner dialogue goes on all day, and continues underground when we fall asleep. This relentless thinking burns a lot of energy and we get exhausted. The more we think the worse we think. Furthermore our thoughts are driven by emotions—usually some low grade variant of fear, anger or desire. These pump hormonal signals through the body saying, "Stay on guard. This is no time to relax!"

Meditation doesn't try to block or process thoughts. It just lets them stream through unattended. Of course, they are very seductive—so the best way to resist temptation is to divert our attention to the sense world.

We instinctively know this anyway. We often use sensual things to distract us from our thoughts and help us relax. When we need a break from work we have a cup of coffee or something to eat. We listen to music, or walk in the park, or play with a cat. When we bite into a cake, the inner dialogue is pushed aside, if only for a few seconds.

Most meditation objects are sensual things—the breath, the body, sounds, music, a repeated word or phrase. Meditation uses this natural principle as a deliberate exercise. If you listened carefully to all the sounds around you for just thirty seconds, for example, you would soon find your habitual mind-chatter had slipped into the background. It doesn't vanish, but you turn down the volume on it, and that's enough. Sensing shifts us from the volatility of thought to the simplicity of just feeling, just seeing, just being.

To summarize, thinking is busy. It is proactive, involving words and concepts of past and future. Thinking usually feels "tight" and is powered by underlying fear, anger or desire. It is exciting but also exhausting. The brain emits the fast arrhythmic "beta" brain waves when we think.

Sensing, however, is quite the opposite. Sensing is passive. It doesn't involve words, or concepts of the past and future. It is emotionally more "loose" and fluid. When sensing, or relaxing, the brain emits the slower and more rhythmic "alpha" brain waves.

Being in the Present

We usually spend very little time in the present—probably about two or three minutes of every hour, on average. We live in our minds, and most of that relates to the past or future. We just check in to the sense world occasionally, so we don't bump into doors or get killed crossing the road.

Meditating, however, draws us into the present. When we simply watch our breath, the past and future temporarily vanish, to our enormous relief. Since most of our anxieties relate to past and future, we can escape them by entering the world of the senses. Often we find the present is a lovely space, full of light and color and beauty that we miss if we are consumed by thought.

We don't have to live permanently in the present and never think of other things. Just spending five to ten minutes of each hour consciously on Planet Earth would be a huge improvement.

If we think too much about past and future, we are bound to be anxious to some degree. Both are frustratingly beyond our control. If we want to be happy, trying to fix up the past or manipulate the future is not the way to go about it.

Passive Awareness

Meditation is sometimes described as the art of pure awareness, or "witnessing" or "just watching" the thoughts and sensations that continually stream through the mind. If the mind is clear and mirror-like, it can dispassionately notice anything without over-responding.

However, meditations based on awareness alone rarely work. It is very difficult to "just watch what arises" unless the mind is stabilized somehow. So awareness meditations usually have a meditation object, such as the breath, at their core. In practice, you focus on the breath while noticing the background thoughts and sensations as well.

The Basic Instructions

To relax, the principles are clear: shift from thinking to sensing, and come into the present moment. Most meditations streamline these principles into simple rules. The core instructions for almost every meditation you will come across, anywhere in the world, are much the same:

1. Focus on a meditation object
2. When the mind wanders away, bring it back
3. Let all other thoughts and sensations pass by

The difference between meditations is in the object chosen to focus on. These are legion, but the underlying principles remain the same. Common objects are the breath, the body, a repeated word or phrase, random sounds, music or visual objects such as flowers, fire or water.

So you focus on your object and gently explore it. Sooner or later, you will find you have jumped the fence and are thinking about something different. Usually this happens unconsciously. It's not a deliberate choice. Once you realize your mind has wandered, however, you can choose.

You can stay with the new thought, which is usually stirring you up. Or you can drop it and return to the meditation object. Each time you release a thought is a moment of liberation. You may do this hundreds of times during a meditation.

Initially, you are either with the meditation object or distracted by something. As you relax, something else happens. You find you can notice thoughts and sensations but they no longer distract you. You are both focused (on the object), and passively aware (of the background thoughts and sensations).

Watching with Detachment

In meditation we don't try to block out thoughts. We just let them stream through in the background. It is said, "You can't stop birds flying overhead, but you can stop them nesting in your hair."

Even in a deep meditation, there are hundreds of subtle thoughts and sensations flowing through the mind each minute. In quick succession you may notice a memory, a slight headache, the sound of traffic, a sense of fatigue, a recurrent problem, an itch. None of these need disturb you one bit. Passive awareness is about accepting the moment just as it is, in all its imperfections. If you don't pursue the mental traffic, you relax anyway.

If we have this "witness" or "spectator" consciousness, we are bound to be peaceful. After all, a spectator just watches the show. He doesn't have to do anything at all. He has a panoramic view, and doesn't get sucked into the dramas.

Focusing and Awareness Work Together

Meditation is the art of putting one thing in the foreground and letting other things pass by in the background. These are the two crucial skills in meditation: focusing and "just watching." You can regard the first as acting like a spotlight, and the second as a floodlight. Both are essential.

Meditators soon realize they can't fix their mind on an object like putting a pound of butter on a table. Within a few seconds the attention will shift to the background as well. It goes on a quick border patrol to check what else is happening. If done lightly and quickly it doesn't break the meditation.

This oscillation between foreground and background, between meditation object and all the rest, is natural and even necessary. Sometimes it happens a lot, sometimes very little. But no matter how hard you try, you can't stop it completely.

In any meditation, you should be practicing both skills. When the mind is focusing, take it deeper. When the mind is patrolling the periphery, "just watch" with real emotional detachment. In time, you may find the detached, clear-seeing, mind is even more valuable than the pleasure of good focus.

A Typical Meditation Session

So what happens in a typical meditation? Normally, people would sit in a quiet space. Many Westerners use an upright padded chair. This is comfortable but also keeps the mind alert. If you are very tense, you could use a reclining chair or lie on the bed. But beware of sleep.

Let us say you are using the breath as your meditation object. Often the mind rebels at first. The unfinished business of the day usually crowds in as soon as you sit down. The first minute or two of a meditation is often quite scrappy as you try to shepherd the mind towards the breath.

Eventually, the mind chatter fades and you start to actually *feel* the breath. You sense it rising and falling, or feel the body expanding and contracting. The breath comes into focus and you notice more detail than you did earlier.

Some meditations are "messy" with lots of thoughts. At other times beautiful mindstates and flashes of insight can arise. After a while, deep peace, mental clarity and profound physical pleasure come so commonly that we start to take them for granted.

Whether a meditation is pleasant or not, you usually feel better for some time afterwards. Even a scruffy meditation can activate the parasympathetic nervous system, lower your energy consumption and put you in touch with yourself again. Your meditation may only have been five minutes long, but its after-effects can linger for an hour or more.

Do You Need to Focus at All?

The idea of focusing can be problematic for people who associate it with knitted brows and a grim determination to get results. In meditation, focusing has a more gentle and non-exclusive quality. Like focusing a camera, it simply puts one thing in the foreground while allowing other thoughts and sensations to be in the background.

Focusing goes hand in hand with pleasure. It occurs naturally when something beautiful attracts us: a cloudscape, a gorgeous body, a flowering bush. When a child is absorbed in a toy, he is focused, sensing and in the present moment—a kind of unconscious meditation.

We develop the skill of focusing because it gives us pleasure. It can't be forced, but it can be encouraged. A gentle curiosity about the object is best. Eventually, the mind wants to focus because the results are so pleasant. The mind becomes clear, awake and in control. This doesn't happen if you just daydream or space out.

Nonetheless, many people want to dispense with focusing (because they feel they can't do it) and jump straight from the busy mind into oblivion. This is like trying to grope your way blindfolded into Paradise. Sometimes you manage it. More commonly, the mind remains at the mercy of thoughts, or subsides into a daydream. The stillness, if attained at all, tends to be soft and vague.

Many teachers also prefer to talk about meditation as a state of space, peace, stillness, silence, or all-embracing emptiness, and discourage the use of focusing to attain this state. However, if you look more closely, there is usually something central in their meditation that serves as a de facto object.

Transcendental Meditation, for example, claims to be a "non-focusing" practice, but it still uses a repeated word to keep the mind settled. Furthermore, non-focusing meditations usually try to evoke a certain mood or effect, which are objects in themselves. Meditations that emphasize space and blankness tend to rely on atmosphere (music, lighting, incense, an instructor's voice) or beautiful ideas to mold the state of mind.

In fact, focusing is the best way to attain a clear, spacious mind because it enables you to both notice and detach from the background thoughts. The object itself tends to takes on a transparent quality. When focusing well, you commonly have a peripheral sense of space, freedom and inner stillness.

In the East, meditation is defined as "one-pointed focus." (It is assumed that tranquility and bliss automatically follow from this.) In the West, however, we tend to associate meditation more with relaxation, daydreaming and a state close to sleep. Consequently, many Westerners "meditate" regularly, but with poor results. They may sit in a kind of dreamy half-sleep for an hour and wonder why they just feel a bit foggy afterwards. This distresses me, because once a person is willing to sit still regularly, it is quite easy to improve their practice. Meditation is all about clear focus (knowing where your mind is) and a dispassionate awareness (of the peripheral activity), and these are easy things to develop.

※

Basic Instructions for All Practices

1. Sit in a relaxed position and loosen the breathing with a couple of sighs.
2. Let your mind gently revolve around the meditation object (e.g., the breath).

3. Be aware of other thoughts and sensations as they call your attention, but don't engage with them. Let them come and go in the background.
4. Enjoy the sensations of the body relaxing.

Or, to put it in a phrase: Focus on one thing and let everything else pass by.

❀

FOUR

A Versatile Skill

❀

Don't Get Stuck at Square One

That image of the seated Buddha has a lot to answer for. We now automatically think of meditation as sitting with eyes closed in a quiet place, focused on something such as the breath. Some people will do just that for years, but it is a very narrow view of meditation.

To meditate you don't need a quiet place. You don't need to be sitting. You don't need your eyes closed. You don't need to stay with one object. You don't even need to be healthy or happy. You just need to be relaxed and aware, whatever you are doing. Easterners were traditionally trained to meditate in every circumstance, even while dying or in the heat of battle, and this versatility suits Westerners as well.

Once you understand how, you can shift your focus from the breath (for example) to anything that catches your fancy. The traditional training would start with sense objects and then move on to images, emotions, ideas and qualities of mind.

Similarly, you would meditate while walking, running, standing and lying down or while doing simple activities, such as cooking, cleaning or gardening. Many people, particularly those who can't sit still, settle their minds much better if they are physically active.

You would also learn to meditate in crises, when you're in noisy places or in pain or stressed to the hilt. You can switch the mind into "passive awareness" mode at a chaotic meeting, or focus for 30 seconds on the flowers on the table. These "spot-meditations" can short-circuit the rising frustration and bring you home to yourself almost immediately.

The Value of Body-based Meditations

The word "meditation" is notoriously vague and covers a multitude of activities. In the West, it often refers to the contemplation of ideas or prayer or creative fantasy or "mind-powers." It is hard to say that any of these have a clear impact on physical health. Furthermore, in the West, the body is commonly regarded as unspiritual and not worthy of attention.

In the East, meditation is more solidly based in the body. Physical relaxation and inner balance are regarded as essential for clarity of mind, and they are given lots of emphasis. In this book, I describe meditation more according to this Eastern approach. If health is important to you, it makes sense to focus on the body, rather than ignoring it.

When you focus a lot on something, you incidentally get to know it quite well. For this reason, meditations based on the breath or the body can be extremely valuable. Any meditation object will relax you, but gaining a deep awareness of the body is an enormous asset if you want to improve your health. I talk extensively about breath- and body-based meditations in Chapters 7 to 9.

As your body-awareness grows, you set up a feedback loop between body and mind. You notice how little shifts in your mind relax the body, which in turn helps the mind let go. For example, you drop an obsessive thought and find that your shoulders drop too. Because this feels good, you let the next thought go as well, and find your breathing softens, and so on.

When focusing on your breath, you are likely to have a peripheral awareness of your changing body chemistry. These signals reassure you that you are meditating well, and tend to speed up the process. Other meditation objects, such as concepts or visualization, will also help you relax, but won't give the accelerated effect of the body/mind feedback.

Probably a majority of the world's millions of meditators focus in some way on the breath or the body. These are very effective practices. In this book, when I want to give a concrete example to illustrate a point, I will use the breath to represent any meditation object. Despite this, the breath and body as meditation objects are not for everyone, nor for every situation.

Almost as popular as the breath is the use of a repeated word or phrase (called an affirmation or "mantra"). These tend to have a slightly hypnotic, chant-like quality that makes them very easy to use.

Both the body-based practices and mantra have a "transparent" quality. They are good mixers. It is quite easy to be aware of the body, for example, while also focusing on sounds or on a visualization or concept.

Which Meditation Object Is Best?

Almost all meditations have the same basic instructions: focus on one thing and let other thoughts and sensations pass by. The difference between them is the object they focus on.

Meditators often get very attached to their particular object. They may feel that the breath meditation is superior to a sound meditation. Or that a particular word or phrase has special qualities. Or that a beautiful visualization is more advanced and spiritual than "just relaxing the body."

In fact, 90% of the benefit of any meditation comes from the degree of focus, not from the object chosen. Deep focus on a twig will clear the mind and relax the body better than a dreamy contemplation of a beautiful idea.

Simple objects usually take you deeper than complex ones. They concentrate and brighten the mind just as a magnifying glass amplifies the power of the sun. More complex objects, on the other hand, tend to refract the energy of the mind. The Tibetans say, "Give simple objects to advanced students and complex ones to beginners" because beginners need more stimulation to hold their attention.

Nonetheless, the object chosen does have a certain effect. It is said, "you become what you meditate on," temporarily. In other words, you pick up some of its mood. Meditating on fire, for example, will have a slightly different effect than meditating on water.

Other Meditation Objects

It is possible to meditate on anything in the sense world—sight, sound, smell, taste or touch. For example, there are at least five ways to meditate on sound. You could listen to music (enjoying it fully, but noticing when you drift away or become distracted). Or you could listen to the random sounds around you (picking out the subtle detail, enjoying the silences).

You could also repeat a word or phrase like a silent chant (feeling the rhythm reverberate in your body). Or you can take a short phrase of music (consciously playing it as a tape loop in your head). In the yogic tradition, you even focus on the subtle humming sounds of the body itself.

You can focus with just as much variety on visual things. The following are all traditional objects: water, fire, the wind in the grass, trees, rocks, space, light, flowers, bones, the primary colors, clouds, the moon . . . and this is just for starters.

Of course, you can also meditate on imagined objects (visualizations, for example), or concepts (like love or forgiveness) or contemplate a problem. These often produce a good emotional tone that is relaxing in itself. Because they are less precise than sensing and typically involve some thought, their effect is often weaker. They usually work best if they piggyback on a basic sensing meditation.

Generally, the simplicity of sense objects leads to greater depth. It is easier to become one-pointed on your heartbeat, for example, than on an elaborate visualization.

Getting off the Meditation Cushion

The Buddha described how to meditate in four separate postures: sitting, walking, standing and lying down. You start, he said, sitting under a tree, focused on the breath. Then you keep this mental quality walking slowly back and forth before your seat. Then you meditate while walking to the village in search of lunch. You meditate while standing outside a house, while people get food for you. Back at your tree, after eating, you meditate while lying on your side (I am sure some of them went to sleep!).

Once you sorted out sitting, walking, standing and lying down as meditation postures, you learned to meditate in every activity—eating, drinking, going to the toilet, getting dressed, and so on. The relaxation comes from just doing what you are doing with awareness—being in the moment, in other words.

Meditation doesn't need to be a trance-like state, oblivious to the world around. We can easily be relaxed and alert while listening to music, watching birds at play, doing yoga or any exercise with awareness, having a shower, eating a peach or arranging flowers. Any posture or any simple activity will do. "I really enjoy the ironing now," said one of my students.

Devising Your Own Practice

Meditation should not stay locked in your quiet room, like a guilty secret. You should take it for a stroll through your day, doing little "spot-meditations" whenever you can. So long as you consciously focus, and notice when the mind is wandering, gardening or art work or preparing food will do fine. Here are some examples:

You can meditate by consciously doing a simple activity. "When I need a break at work," a bank manager told me, "I have a glass of water." And she makes it a deliberate meditation exercise. She feels the touch of the plastic cup, listens to the trickle of the water, tastes each sip slowly and hears the empty cup fall into the bin. She is in the present, focused on sensation.

You can meditate while exercising. "I meditate while swimming," said another student. "I focus on each breath, making it full and rhythmic, and watch the bubbles as I breathe out. Sometimes I say a mantra as well, to blow the words away. Swimming used to be so boring," she added. "But now the time flies by."

You could focus on the sensations around you at random. "I just try to be in the present," said another student. "My husband and I were camping in the desert recently. In the evenings, I watched the shadows creeping across the landscape and the smoke rising from the barbecue and heard the food cooking. I listened to the birds and the sound of the wind in the trees. I consciously focused on one sensation after another."

You can even meditate on unpleasant things. "I meditate best with pain," said a student with cancer. "It often becomes so intense, I have to lie down and focus on it. I scan my body from top to bottom, telling myself, 'It's okay to let go now.' The pain always fades when I meditate on it."

One woman told me, "When my kids were little, I used to lie on the couch in the afternoon to rest. My eyes were closed and my body was resting, but I stayed awake. I kept track of the kids by listening to the sounds they made." She was relaxed, but her mind was still alert. By focusing on sound, she could have a rest while still making sure the kids were safe.

Spot-Meditations

A meditation can literally be just a few seconds long. "I was waiting to pick up my child outside the school," said one woman. "He was late as usual, so I meditated. I decided to watch the raindrops running down the windscreen. It was very soothing. I was sorry to stop when he turned up."

It only takes ten seconds, focusing deeply on something in the sense world, to extract yourself from thought. You can look at a houseplant or a tree outside your office window. You can give full attention to the next sip of tea. Ten seconds is all it takes to slow the brain waves down.

Once you get the principles of meditation clear, you have enormous freedom in how you apply them. It's a luxury to be able to meditate during boring lectures or meetings. You can drop the physical stress while standing in line at the bank, or while taking a shower. At any time, you can switch into observer mode—able to "just watch" your thoughts and emotions dispassionately.

If we just think of meditation as "sitting with closed eyes in a quiet place," it is limited to a formal activity you can only do a few minutes each day. But if you think of it as a relaxed and aware quality of mind, you can integrate it fully into your day. All you need is a few conscious breaths to activate it.

Can You Meditate Automatically?

People often ask me, "Is daydreaming (or running or watching TV) a kind of meditation?" The answer is no. The state may be similar to that produced by meditation—relaxed and alert—but it arose inadvertently. Meditation is always a conscious discipline. Even in the depths of trance, you should know what you are doing and be able to steer it.

Often we can be relaxed and alert without needing to meditate at all, but these peaceful moments don't come as often as we would like. Simply to do what we like is no guarantee. We can't just stroke the cat, or walk in the park, and immediately hope to feel good. If we are upset, the mind will ramble and fuss, whatever we do. We can walk all the way through the park and be aware of nothing but our thoughts and obsessions.

We all have strategies to relax, but they are often slow and inef-fective. Meditation, however, is fast. It is the art of relaxing quickly and consciously, whenever you want to and in any circumstances. Some people may take five hours to wind down after a demanding day at work. A meditator can shed the thoughts and relax the body to the point of sleep in five minutes.

Learning to Meditate

Meditation is not complicated, but it is much easier to learn from a human being than from a book. A teacher and a group are likely to give you vital non-verbal clues about how to go about it.

A regular schedule is useful, but not essential. If you make it a habit of meditating at a certain time each day, you are less likely to let it be squeezed aside by other priorities.

Usually it is best to get proficient at one or two techniques before you branch out to others. This way, when you sit down to meditate you automatically slip into your basic practice rather than wondering what to do.

You can do your meditation "cold," or you can amplify the effect with various props and rituals. You can have a shower first, do some preparatory exercise or create an attractive atmosphere with incense, soft music and lighting if you wish. If you have real difficulty relaxing, these props can be helpful. Even lie on your bed if you have to.

Without being hard on yourself, learn to evaluate your medita-tion. Notice if you are relaxing at all. Know the difference between daydreaming and focusing. Notice when you are indulging thoughts rather than gently detaching from them. Discuss what you are doing with other meditators, or with a teacher if you can find one.

When you are able to relax quickly and clear the mind of unnec-essary thought, don't get stuck on just one practice. Improvise and learn to carry that relaxed and alert quality into the rest of your day.

✳

Red Light Meditation

This "spot-meditation" works best if you are late and in a hurry and the traffic lights turn red just as you approach.

If you feel frustrated and annoyed, smile to yourself. You have been given perhaps a whole minute to stop and do nothing. One whole minute to breathe softly.

Let yourself sigh deeply, lingering on the out-breath. Check your body for excess tension. How are you holding the steering wheel? Are your face and neck muscles tighter than they need to be? Settle back into the seat and let your belly soften. Breathe consciously.

This exercise finishes as the light turns green. Now devote all your attention to the task at hand: driving safely. And look forward to the next red light.

PART TWO

Healing the Body

PART TWO

✸

FIVE

The Cardiovascular System

✸

With certain ailments such as cancer, the link between stress and ill-health is somewhat indirect. With cardiovascular problems, however, the dynamics are obvious and the evidence is clear: stress is a major contributor to heart disease.

The good news is that you can therefore do something about it. By meditating, for example, you can lower your blood pressure on the spot. And by de-stressing in general, you reduce the danger factors.

People have long tried to find causal links between certain personality types and specific diseases. Extensive research has now dispelled most of these hypotheses with one exception. People who habitually feel and express anger commonly get heart disease—probably because of elevated levels of stress hormones in the blood.[1]

How Sudden Stress Can Kill You

The stress response is designed to massively increase available energy in the body as preparation for fight or flight. The cardiovascular system is the major engine and delivery system for this. During a stress response it works many times harder than when we are at rest.

It all starts with a perception, real or imagined, of danger. The hypothalamus tells the pituitary to tell the adrenals to release adrenaline and glucocorticoids into the bloodstream. The full sympathetic nervous system response accelerates the heart rate and respiration, constricts the veins and arteries, and makes the blood thick with fatty acids and glycogen.

This alone can kill you, if you're vulnerable. In a heart attack or a stroke the blood vessels can burst under the increased pressure alone. A sudden spike of extreme fear, anger or terror can kill you on the spot. Even birds and animals, who suffer less than we do from chronic hypertension, can die this way.

How Chronic Stress Affects the Arteries

However, the real damage is caused by years of chronic stress. We now know why and how the cardiovascular system breaks down. The stress response is designed to last only a few minutes. Ideally we would fight or flee, the cholesterol would be consumed and we would return to a state of balance. When stressed, our heart rate increases to deliver the energy-rich blood to the body faster. For the same reason, the tiny circular muscles around the blood vessels contract, since a narrow tube squirts a fluid faster than a wide one. The blood itself is more viscous as it carries the extra fatty acids and sugars.

So the accelerated heart is pumping a more viscous fluid through narrower passages much faster than usual. This is a high-revving body —like driving a car at fifty miles an hour in second gear. It's not surprising it often breaks down.

Firstly, the increased pressure of the blood can cause tiny rips in the lining of the arteries. Secondly, the thicker blood carries more semi-solid blobs of fatty acids within it, which scour the walls and increase the damage. Particularly vulnerable are the places where the arteries branch into the ever tinier vessels that feed the individual cells of the body.[2]

Stress hormones increase the blood's tendency to clot.[3] When damage occurs, fatty acids and blood platelets get under the lining, coagulate and seal the damage. Every piece of repair work, however, is bulky and juts into the passageway, making it a little narrower and increasing the overall pressure.

Micro-deaths and Full-blown Attacks

The scene is now set for real damage. A clot will often break loose and block a small arteriole. Within seconds, all those downstream cells will suffocate and die.[4] These micro-deaths or "infarcts" seem to be quite common in older people. If a large clot breaks loose, it can jam in a larger vessel and cause a major attack.

The same culprit that makes the bullet also makes the gun. Chronic hypertension, by tearing the lining, makes the clot form in the first place and a peak of rage or fear, by increasing the heart rate, blasts the clot loose to inflict mayhem downstream.

Heart attacks are dramatic, but the real cause is the years of hypertension, which day by day degrades the cardiovascular system without our even noticing it. So if you have hypertension, what can you do to help—besides diet, exercise and drugs? In brief, anything that helps you relax will deactivate the sympathetic nervous system and bring you back to balance. Quite simply, the more relaxed you are during the day, the more you care for your heart.

Hypertension and Tight Muscles Go Together

There are many meditations that require no awareness of the body at all. However, to improve your health, I encourage you to read your body signals in detail. Some people can actually feel when their blood pressure is high—as a thumping in the chest or head—but most of us can't. So we have to focus on the next best thing: our muscular tension. If our musculature is tight, we can reasonably assume that our cardiovascular system is under pressure too. They operate in tandem, and the stress response affects them equally.

Tension is all-pervasive. It goes all the way through to the muscles of the colon, the groin, the eyebrows and also the tiny muscles around the blood vessels. This rigid musculature impinges on the thousands of little tubes and pipes that are the circulatory system, and doesn't allow them to expand and contract fully as the blood pumps through. The blood has to struggle in obstructed fashion through a stiff and unresponsive body. The result: high blood pressure.

Relaxing the Musculature for the Heart's Sake

If you realize you are unnecessarily tense, it is surprisingly easy to change it. It is not hard to take a few deep breaths and let yourself settle, once you know how. This will deactivate the stress response within seconds.

The first stage in releasing tensions is to actually acknowledge them. In other words, we no longer try to ignore them. Stress tends to numb the body via the pain-killing effects of endorphins and enkephalins. This is called "stress-induced analgesia."[5] When we relax, these natural painkillers fade and we feel the body as it is. In fact, a heightened awareness of the aches and pains in the body usually tells us we have activated the relaxation response.

It is useful to notice the process that muscles go through as they relax. If we stop resisting the little aches and pains that go with tension, they usually get more obvious, then expand and then gradually dilute. Soon, we realize the neck pain that bothered us five minutes ago has all but gone.

We also start to notice the difference between a tight and a relaxed body. A tight body feels hard and rigid, with points of discomfort. A relaxed body, however, feels softer and more flowing, even if it is not entirely pain-free. Residual discomforts usually feel more fluid than stuck.

As we relax, our musculature softens and the arteries become more supple and elastic. The blood becomes less viscous and the pressure reduces. You may also notice a slight warmth or tingling on the skin. When we relax, the blood is partially redirected from the big muscles to the extremities and the digestive system.

Tense muscles are out of balance and relaxation returns them to homeostasis. Once you meditate, you start to recognize this feeling. It is subtle, but you can say the body feels alive, soft and flowing, with a gentle tingling energy throughout. It is very quiet, but also rather warm and contented. It is quite different from the feeling of habitual tension.

Meditation is the process of retraining the musculature. If you meditate regularly, you soon realize that certain muscles are tighter than they need to be. When you notice the tension, you can loosen it. The improvement may be minimal (and you may still feel tense at the end of the meditation). However, hundreds of minimal releases start to add up over time. The bucket fills, drop by drop.

How Hypertensive People Relax

Hypertension is usually the habit of decades. Hypertensive people are often type-A achievers, who look and feel stiff. As such, the level of muscular tension they feel seems normal to them. They do relax, but not very much.

Some people recognize this when they say, "I've always been tight. I never relax." However, everyone can improve their level of internal suppleness. Even a 10% reduction in tension will have huge benefits.

Hypertensive people are often determined and disciplined people (that can be part of their problem!). So I find they actually practice their meditation and soon get the knack of it. Each day they feel fractionally more relaxed. They often get good at spot-meditations, which fit more easily into a type-A schedule.

They are programming themselves to act in a less manic way, not just when they meditate, but through the whole day. It may be unfamiliar to them, but they learn to take things more easily and be a bit softer around the edges. They are shifting their personality type from A to A-minus. By modifying their behavior and habits of response, they indirectly improve their blood pressure.

I find this usually takes about a month, but the results can be dramatic. Many of my students have dropped their systolic reading around forty points over that period. Herbert Benson more cautiously reports, "our studies and others show that the relaxation response can lower blood pressure by about 5 to 10 millimeters of mercury in people with hypertension."[6]

Breath and body awareness practices are usually the best for people with hypertension (see Chapters 7–8). Since they are retraining their musculature, it helps to use the body itself as a meditation object. Nonetheless, any meditation that simplifies their mental activity and makes their mind less active will be useful.

✺

"Am I Relaxed?"

You can ask yourself this question anywhere—at a meeting, standing in line, while listening to a friend, doing the dishes, walking downstairs. You'll often find you're carrying unnecessary tension—burning more energy than you need for the task at hand.

At this moment, you are reading a book. If you ask yourself the above question, you might notice you are not as relaxed as you might be. Possibly you are holding your breath, or your posture is knotted up or your muscles are rigid.

Take a deep breath or two to release the breathing. Now soften the muscles of the face, the shoulders, and the belly just by noticing where you are unnecessarily tense. Count ten breaths (without trying to control them), while noticing how your body feels.

Notice how much tension you can release in the space of a minute or two. Now continue reading while keeping a background awareness of your body.

CORE INSTRUCTIONS

1. Anywhere, anytime, ask the question, "Am I relaxed?"
2. Notice how you are sitting and breathing.
3. Adjust your posture to relieve tension.
4. Consciously let go on the outbreath, 5 or 10 times.

Resume what you were doing, staying in touch with your body.

❀

SIX

A Healthy Musculature

❀

The benefits of a supple musculature are almost impossible to over-estimate. The muscles of a healthy child are soft, supple and strong. This ability of muscles to expand and contract fully, as they do in a child, is the epitome of good health. Every cell of the body benefits from healthy muscle function.

When we get stressed, we tend to notice it most clearly in our muscles: they get tight. Stress causes contraction of big and small muscles throughout the body, leading to that "coiled spring" feeling. In the last chapter I showed how relaxing the musculature helps the cardiovascular system. In this chapter I outline how muscle tension affects the muscles themselves, as well as the rest of the body.

Stress molds our posture. Many physical therapists can read a person's life history of stress just by looking at the body. This is how it works: Tension makes muscles contract and become shorter. If we don't relax fully (and who does?) they remain partly contracted, even in deep sleep. By middle age, we find we are bound by thousands of muscular straps that get tighter and shorter each year.

For example, worry makes the neck and shoulder muscles tighten, pulling the shoulders forwards. When we're young, our posture is gracefully erect, but by middle age this habit of worry can permanently hunch the upper back. Occasionally we see an older person who has retained the suppleness of youth and we realize that a tight, restricted body is not an inevitable consequence of aging. Our minds are doing this to us.

Tense muscles burn a lot of energy to stay that way, so they get fatigued and we under-use them. Chronically tight muscles are painful, suffer injury readily, atrophy and eventually die. Muscle tension and fatigue are such common companions of sickness and disease, it is hard to say which comes first.

Tight muscles impede the flow of blood, nutrients and chemical messengers to cells and organs. In effect, they slowly strangle the body. Many systems in the body, such as breathing, peristalsis and blood circulation, depend on rhythmic muscle contraction and expansion. A tight musculature clamps down on these and makes their work harder. Because a tense body is less internally mobile, the organs do not get the ambient movement they need to maintain good function. Let us look at all this in more detail.

Tight Muscles Are Prone to Injury

When a sudden load is put on a tight muscle, it is more likely to tear than stretch. These injuries are often so tiny we barely notice them, but the effect can radiate outwards. Once a muscle is injured, the adjacent muscles stiffen around it to act as a splint, which makes them also prone to injury.

Chronically tight muscles may continually suffer such micro-injuries, and be progressively weakened by expanding areas of scar tissue. This is commonly the scenario behind lower back pain, for example.

On the other hand, we may not feel any specific point of pain. We just feel stiff and sore in general. Tight muscles don't function well and don't feel good. Because of our micro-injuries, we start to move cautiously, like old people, to avoid hurting ourselves.

The body quickly atrophies if we don't move enough. After just a few weeks in a plaster caste, the muscles of a leg will have visibly shrunken. In time the tissue will start dying, and the muscles never recover their full function—it's gone forever. Did those muscles decide, like some old people do, they no longer had any reason to go on living? It is as if they thought, "Movement hurts too much. I'm not going to move any longer."

Tight Muscles Starve the Cells

Healthy muscles relax and contract fully many times a day. Blood can flow easily through muscles like these. Supple muscles are well-aerated and supplied with plentiful nutrients. The cells receive enough oxygen to metabolize the energy they need to function well.

In contrast, a tight muscle remains contracted. The tiny passageways for the blood are squeezed. At a certain point, the blood cells can't get through. The tightest parts of a muscle are like a fortified city. When the gates are closed, supplies can't get in, and waste products can't get out. The muscle is starved of nutrients and poisoned by its own waste products.

It's not just the muscles that suffer. If the body is rigid, the blood can't carry oxygen, nutrients and other vital products as freely through the veins and arteries. All the organs of the body, not just the muscles, can suffer from reduced rations. If your body is sick or trying to fight disease, a tense or inactive body is cutting off the supply lines.

Slowly Dying from Asphyxiation

Dr. Sherwin Nuland, the author of *How We Die*, tells of an elderly lady who told her doctor, "Death keeps taking little bits of me." She was literally correct. It can be argued that the fundamental cause of cell, organ, and whole-body death is lack of oxygen. Nuland quotes a renowned doctor as saying, "Death may be due to a wide variety of diseases and disorders, but in every case the underlying physiological cause is a breakdown in the body's oxygen cycle."[1]

When the flow of oxygen into a cell sinks below a certain critical level, or if an upstream arteriole has been obstructed by a blood clot, the cell dies. A person who has suffered several heart attacks, for example, may have a lot of scar tissue (dead cells) in the heart muscle, where the oxygen supplies were cut off. The same process may happen on a smaller scale hundreds of times in an aging body. These "infarcts" or micro-strokes destroy cells almost invisibly, and riddle the body with scar tissue.

Scar tissue, of course, can no longer do the work of living tissue. If some of the muscle tissue in an organ dies, the remaining tissues have to work harder to compensate. In the heart muscle, for example, this leads to strain and a general state of ongoing emergency.

Inner Mobility Is Essential for Health

To be healthy, muscles need to be used, for their own sake and for the rest of the body. It is deadly to sit too much. Our health depends on continual movement. We were not made to sit in chairs and cars all day.

It's easy to say that muscular relaxation is good, and tension is bad, but it's not that simple. Tight muscles aren't elastic enough to function well, but under-used muscles atrophy and die. Too much inactivity is not only bad for the body. It also makes us feel miserable.

While sick people get the advice, "Just lie in bed and rest," this can be the worst thing for them. It is good for their body and their spirits to struggle out of bed and putter slowly around the house. When we're sick it is best to be as mobile as possible without depleting our reserves.

People who are bedridden know the problems of insufficient movement. If we don't walk, for example, the blood and lymph pool in our feet. Walking pumps it all back up the body. A healthy musculature acts as our 24-hour-a-day masseur.

In reality, the inner organs and glands, the nervous system and skeletal structure, all need to be regularly massaged and exercised each day by movement. Each breath, for example, gently lowers and raises the liver. Each movement of the arm stretches the veins and nerves.

This may be one reason why women, who are usually more active over the years, tend to age better than men.

Body Functions Are Inhibited

Many of our body processes depend on rhythms of tension and release. If we are chronically tight, the muscles work in a narrow, limited spectrum and often lose their rhythm altogether. In particular, our lymphatic system, digestion and breathing suffer.

Our lymphatic system, which fights infections and removes waste products, doesn't have a pump like the heart. Its network of tubes and glands is completely dependent on adjacent muscular activity to move the lymph along. If this becomes stagnant through inactivity, it is less capable of fighting disease and more vulnerable to being infected by the pathogens it is trying to destroy.

The digestive system is very psychosomatic. The stomach literally locks up within seconds when you are alarmed, to divert energy to the fight-or-flight response. It stays shut down until you relax, which is the only time we digest food efficiently. We all know that swallowing and evacuation can become difficult if we are tense.

Peristalsis, the muscular activity that moves food through the tract, works by continuous contraction and expansion. When tense, the muscles only contract and the process grinds to a crawl. Furthermore, peristalsis is designed to work in a supple belly, not a rigid one. Tight muscles, both in the digestive system and in the body around it, make us more likely to suffer from digestive problems.

When the body is tight, our breathing becomes increasingly shallow and jerky. The range of the diaphragm is limited, which disables adequate uptake of oxygen and expulsion of carbon dioxide. The pooling of stagnant air in the lungs creates a moist breeding ground for bacteria. The combination of shallow breathing and poor heart function leads to the respiratory problems that particularly affect the elderly. (I will discuss breathing in more detail in Chapter 8.)

Relaxing Muscles to Help the Whole Body

Obviously, tight musculature is not the sole cause of heart disease, indigestion, pain, pneumonia and premature old age. I place so much emphasis on it because this is one thing we can consciously improve. Because the body is profoundly interconnected, working with one system benefits the rest.

Our nervous systems operate as an elaborate feedback network of chemical, electrical and somatic messages. If we relax our musculature and restore it to balance, we know we have activated the relaxation response. This works not just on the muscles, but everywhere. Sympathetic and parasympathetic activity are global events in the body. As the musculature relaxes, the rest of the body returns to balance as well.

We can directly control some things in the body and mind. Most things we can't. We can't directly lower blood pressure or the secretion of adrenaline, for example. But we can do things that indirectly have that effect. By meditating—shifting into a passive awareness, and focusing on something simple—we activate the relaxation response. This in turn releases muscle tension, which we can partially feel.

Beyond our awareness, however, the heart rate and adrenaline levels also return to normal when we relax. Without our sensing it, blood lactate levels drop, the immune system functions better, digestion swings back into action, and so on.

The secret of relaxing well is to have a heightened awareness of the process. The more aware we become, the more we can direct the process, fine-tune it, pick up the danger signals and do what is needed immediately. This means we stay close to allostatic balance—most of the time at least.

While few of us can recover the suppleness of our youth, we can make huge steps in the right direction by learning to relax at will. When we meditate, we notice the concrete in our shoulders turning back into living flesh. The effect filters down to the thousands of muscles, big and small, around the body. Sensitive meditators often feel this process as a ripple of subtle sensations as the micro-knots untie and the juices start to flow again. The pain and stiffness go, and our bodies become comfortable places to inhabit once again.

Acknowledging How Tense You Are

Many people don't even realize they are tense at all, let alone recognize the feeling of relaxation. Tension usually releases in stages, the first of which is to actually notice it. The next stage is to know where you hold your tension, and what it feels like. Then you need to notice (or admit) how tense you actually are. If you try to skip these stages, and just "get rid of" your tension quickly, it won't work, I guarantee it.

Tension can be surprisingly easy to ignore. We distract ourselves with talking or entertainment or overwork or drugs. Eventually we get so exhausted we fall asleep and become unconscious of everything. However, this doesn't cure the problem any more than taking morphine cures cancer.

Habitually ignoring tension often leads to a kind of numbness. Many people feel very little between neck and feet, aside from obvious pain. They may not feel too bad, but they don't feel that good either. Unfortunately, tension usually gets worse the longer you ignore it.

It is said that if you drop a frog into hot water it will jump out. But if you put the frog in cold water and slowly heat it, it will stay there and die. Similarly, our tension creeps up on us over the years. We get so accustomed to high tension that it seems normal. We assume we are relaxed if the stress reading slides down from "extreme" to merely "high."

People tend to notice their mounting tension gradually. They notice their stomach is always upset, they are not sleeping well, they are irritable and not enjoying life, and ordinary tasks seem all too much.

Sometimes the tension reaches a toxic level and bursts explosively into your attention. It seems appropriate that heart attacks and cancers often erupt out of these hidden spaces. One way or the other, people eventually realize, "I'm just so tense. I can't ignore it any longer. I've got to do something about this."

Recognizing the Tension in Detail

The next stage is to identify the problem—to notice exactly where we hold our tension. Shoulders and stomachs are favorite places, but almost anywhere will do.

There is the "headache band" that rings the head from forehead to neck. Some of us clench the jaw muscles, or the eyes are tight and strained. Some choke in the chest, or around the heart. Others lock the diaphragm, or clamp up the genitals. Some people have solid thighs that get painfully jumpy when they relax.

Tension can be literally anywhere in the body—even in the tongue or toes. But while people often know of their favorite spot, they don't recognize all the secondary places where they lock up. Tension, after all, goes everywhere the muscles do. There can be a virtual "Gulag Archipelago" of prison camps hidden away around the body.

Our total tension is built up from thousands of small points of tension. They can all go in time, but they won't all dissolve in the first three minutes of a relaxation exercise. Some tensions are quite momentary. The facial muscles, for example, tighten as you speak and usually relax as you listen. Other tensions last longer. The stress of a busy day can last a few hours into the evening but largely dissolves during sleep.

Some tensions may have been building for months, as difficulties at work or home accumulate. In these cases, you wake in the morning still carrying the tight shoulders or knotted stomach of yesterday.

Some tensions may have been around for years—the stiff back or fixed smile for example. However, any tension, no matter how brief, that outlives its usefulness is bad for us.

Awareness Has a Magical Effect

Strange to say, the more you recognize your tension, the more you relax. Ignoring it and trying to feel good just doesn't work. A little awareness is good, but a heightened awareness helps enormously. Awareness has an almost magical effect. If you touch the small painful places in your body with love and acceptance, they respond. Your body knows how to relax if you give it the chance to do so.

For example, if you notice you are gritting your teeth or clenching your fist, they start to release almost immediately. You don't even need a technique (though that certainly helps). The awareness alone is enough to get the process started.

Yet this is still hard to do, and we rarely relax fully. And feeling a little better is not the same as relaxing deeply. We release the breath, drop the shoulder, unclench the fists, but the sensations are a bit distasteful. We are often annoyed with ourselves for feeling the way we do. For this reason, consciously releasing tight muscles is not as effective as meditation, which works by defusing the underlying emotions. The next chapter introduces our first major meditation practice: scanning the body.

❀

SEVEN

Body-scanning Meditations

❀

There are thousands of possible meditation objects, but if you choose to focus on the body, it has a double-whammy effect. Not only does the mind focus, but you also see the physical benefits immediately. This is most reassuring and often accelerates the process. For this reason, I strongly recommend body-scanning practices for people concerned with their health. Almost as good are the meditations on the breath and on pain discussed later.

Muscle relaxation methods are often taught by doctors and psychologists who know nothing of formal meditation practice. "Muscle relaxation decreases or prevents muscle spasm, reduces or controls muscle tension and helps control other physiological mechanisms involved in nervous system arousal and pain production. Muscle relaxation may also reduce anxiety and distress, improve sleep and distract a person from the pain."[1]

Progressive Muscle Relaxation is a famous Western method in which you contract and relax parts of the body in turn. This does work, but it is more busy than it needs to be. To meditate, you only need to focus on one thing and let other thoughts and sensations pass by. You don't need to "make the body relax." This happens naturally when you focus.

By not trying to "do" anything, meditation dissolves the mental effort that make us tense. Body-scanning usually relieves tension better than exercise or Progressive Muscle Relaxation, because it shifts the underlying mindstate. Passively sensing the body is much less stressful that trying to make it relax. If anxiety is making the body tense, no amount of yoga or tensing and relaxing will make it truly supple.

The Effect of Scanning

In the main practice below, you scan the body gently from top to bottom, or vice versa. You use the changing sensations in each place— pulsing, pressure, tension, or whatever—to stop your attention from wandering. This tends to bring the gross and subtle tensions to the surface of consciousness, and alleviates many of them within seconds. It is rather like combing the knots out of a tangle of long hair.

Since you are focusing on the body, you actually notice what happens. You start to breathe again, and the pressures of the day drop from your face. Gradually, the deeper tensions and chronic rigidities come to the surface and loosen their grip. You feel the big and small muscles softening throughout the body. As the adrenaline charge fades, the limbs start to feel heavy. You may feel the increased blood flow to the extremities as warmth or tingling on the skin.

With more sensitivity, you can pick up other downstream effects of the relaxation response: subtle breathing, more life in the digestive system, a sense of warmth and flow through every part. The "energy-field" (the network of sensations in the body) becomes more soft, supple, fluid and alive. It is easy to imagine you are nourishing all the cells of the body, just by sitting still and doing nothing.

A meditator can illuminate the body from within. Many of my generation of meditators were taught to spend a whole hour doing just one scan of the body from top to toe, or vice versa. It is extraordinary how entertaining this can be. The body is alive with sensation—tingling, pulsing, pressure, pain, bliss, the ebb and flow of the breath. It continually changes according to the activity of the mind and the depth of meditation.

By scanning the body, we often notice the emotions that accompany our tension. Our tight neck muscles bring up frustration, or our lower back pain raises despair. Chest pain or physical discomfort may be interwoven with anger or resentment. Fortunately, both the physical and emotional pain tend to release if you "just watch" them.

The meditation process often results in a deep sense of pleasure. It still surprises me that physical bliss can coexist with the inevitable discomfort of having a living body. People often say that severe pain or illness are no obstacles to being relaxed and mentally clear.

A heightened sensitivity to the body can be both enjoyable and therapeutic. While most meditators have a reasonable degree of body-awareness, some make it their speciality. This can have such extraordinary benefits that I am inclined to say body-awareness meditations are the most powerful of all healing techniques.

Because scanning is so therapeutic, people often try too hard to fix each place and make it feel good. This rarely works, and can lead to frustration. The best kind of focus involves a gentle acceptance, and even love, of the body, just as it is. This is what gives it permission to relax. It is good to remember that we can't directly control the relaxation response. All we can do is focus without expectations. When the mind settles, the body automatically lets go.

In this practice, you scan slowly from top to bottom or vice versa. It can be done "plain," or with the addition of visualizations, mantras or affirmations. There are many possibilities.

❊

Body-scanning

First sit comfortably and shake your body loose, releasing any obvious tension. Take a couple of deep breaths and let go completely as you breathe out.

Scan the body at your own speed, noticing the subtle detail. You can count the breaths if you wish, spending perhaps four, or eight or ten breaths in each region.

1. Scalp and forehead
(Notice tingling, pulsing, pressure ...)
2. The face and lower part of the head
(Soften the eyes. Let the mouth and jaw go slack)
3. Neck, throat, shoulders, arms and hands
(Like stroking or massaging the body with your mind)
4. Chest and upper back
(Feel the lungs expand and contract)
5. Diaphragm and solar plexus
(Feel the movement of the lower ribs)
6. The belly and lower back
(Feel the soft organs move slightly as you breathe)
7. Hips, legs and feet
(Feel or imagine the breath dropping through your body)

Now let your mind rest wherever it's attracted to in the body. Watch the breath or the heartbeat or any other sensation in that place. Stay there as long as you like or scan again, either up or down. Enjoy the feeling of the body relaxing.

BREATHING THROUGH THE BODY

Body-scanning lends itself to variations. If you have a more tactile disposition, you may prefer to imagine you are "breathing through" the body, or massaging each part of it with the breath. You gently comb out the tensions as you go. If you can feel your heartbeat, you can imagine it gently pulsing through every part of the body.

WHITE LIGHT

A common practice is the "white light" meditation. This means you "massage" the body from top to bottom with light. It could be soft golden light, like nectar or milk and honey. It could be a sparkling crystalline light, or a cool blue light, or a warm pink light. Be kinesthetic and feel it flowing especially into the painful places. Let the light have texture and aroma and even sound. You can amplify the effect by saying an affirmation such as "Love" or "Peace" or "Health" on each out-breath.

If you wish, you can imagine the light caressing your organs, flesh and bones. Feel it going through the brain, the nervous system, throat, lungs, heart, intestines, liver, kidneys, sexual organs, the spine, buttocks, arms, legs and feet. This "mind-massage" evokes a feeling of affectionately caring for yourself.

CHAKRAS

In this meditation you let your mind rest in the central point of each of the seven regions listed on the previous page. You stay in each place until it feels loose and open, and move on to the next. This is the process of "opening the chakras" and can be combined with an affirmation. You may also like to imagine a point of sparkling light or a particular color in each center.

EIGHT

Breathing Easily

When we are sick, we often feel "This is a crisis! I've got to do something." We frantically research our illness, check out treatment options, take vitamin and herbal supplements, talk to people and try to make lifestyle changes we hope will help.

This busyness and mental turmoil can be just as damaging as the actual illness. "Not doing" is just as important as "doing" when we are sick. We often fail to do what would help the most: we don't relax.

To restore balance, we need to notice when we are tense. If you get into the habit of checking, "Right now, am I relaxed or am I tense?" usually you will know. If you are tense, there may be all kinds of signs— rigid body, anxious mind, aching shoulders, knotted stomach.

However, the clearest indicator of all is the breath. It gives you an instant printout on how tense or relaxed you are in that moment. If your breathing is locked up, there is no way you can pretend you are completely okay. In general, loose, open breathing is a sign of relaxation and pleasure, and the opposite is a sign of stress.

When stressed, our breathing becomes jerky and tight. The muscles that line the airways tighten and compromise the breath flow. The mucus layer of the tract thickens (the histamine effect) and makes breathing more difficult. People who are sick or tense or aging typically expel air from the lungs less and less efficiently. This leads to a pooling of moist air in the lungs, inhibiting uptake of oxygen and damaging the delicate alveoli. These damp stagnant conditions are ideal breeding grounds for respiratory infections. Inadequate respiration, like muscular tension, is a major contributor to ill health.

The Breath as Master Switch

Fortunately the breath, like muscle tension, is within our voluntary control. When stressed, we can use the breath to initiate the relaxation response and restore the whole body to homeostasis. Yoga practitioners often regard the breath as the key to health and longevity.

We can relax our breathing more readily than we can release tight stomach muscles, for example. The effect of six or seven conscious outbreaths can be remarkable. This alone can defuse the tension, lower the metabolic rate a few notches and shift the body towards a healthier state. It wouldn't hurt to do this several times a day.

Scanning profoundly relaxes the body, but it can take some time. The breath, however, is like the master switch in a household. When you free up the breathing, the whole body responds. It is not as subtle but you get results within seconds.

Checking in to your breathing is like coming home. It doesn't matter if you are in an office or the street or in an argument. You can listen to your body anywhere, anytime, in the space of a breath or two.

The breath is where our conscious mind interfaces with the instinctive life of the body. Breathing is both a voluntary and involuntary activity. Neither our conscious minds nor our bodies have exclusive control of the breath. For this reason, we don't use the breath to "make ourselves relax," or force ourselves to "breathe well." It is better to cooperate with the natural rhythms and irregularities of the breath.

Watching the Breath Leads to Easier Breathing

Meditating on the breath has two huge benefits. It relaxes the whole body and it loosens up the breathing itself. I regard the former as primary. If the body relaxes, the breathing will automatically improve.

However, if you try to "breathe well," you may find the effort prevents you from relaxing.

Once you learn how, it's not hard to be relatively relaxed all day, which usually results in good respiration. Useful as conscious breathing is, we can't do it all day long. The effort would interfere with our other activities. Being relaxed, however, only requires that you pay attention to what you are doing, and then the breathing follows.

"Just watching" the breath will improve respiration, and the benefits are huge. Although oxygen is the rocket fuel that powers every cell in the body, we take it for granted. If you suffer ongoing fatigue, you may think, "I need more iron" (to transport oxygen around the body). You may just need more oxygen.

As we relax, the body opens up and our breathing becomes fuller. When we relax completely, homeostasis is restored, which means the body is taking in precisely the amount of oxygen it needs—not too much (which would stimulate the body), nor too little (which would starve it).

The feeling of health and vigor goes hand in hand with good breathing. Whenever we exercise or do hard physical work, we are forced to breathe more deeply than usual. This lifts our spirits and makes our skin glow. We never feel depressed after exercise or moderate physical work.

Conversely, when we are tense or sick we usually under-breathe, and virtually shut down the breathing for many minutes at a time. This physiological depression can be reflected by mental depression. Reduced breathing often goes hand in hand with inactivity, anxiety and despair.

Respiratory Problems

People with asthma find meditation very helpful. This became vividly clear to me on one of my meditation retreats. An asthmatic student realized she had left her inhaler at home and was about to return for it. She normally used it fifteen times a day.

Since home was nearby, I suggested she delay the trip until she really needed to. As it turned out, she felt so relaxed the whole weekend that it wasn't necessary. That was her first weekend free of Ventolin for years!

The scientific research has proved that meditation opens constricted air passages. In particular, the relaxation response opens up the tight muscles around the throat. It also reverses the aggravating effects of histamine and mucus buildup in the bronchioles, which reduce the air space in an asthma attack.[1]

An asthmatic often finds her breathing somewhat uncomfortable. It feels raspy or constricted, and can trigger the negative feelings she has toward the illness itself. Consequently, to avoid those sensations she tries to breathe as little as possible, which makes matters worse.

When people with respiratory problems learn to meditate, they notice how much better their breathing feels. As they become familiar with the feeling of relaxed breathing they will be able to return to it when they need it.

People with respiratory problems often benefit from different kinds of controlled breathing. If at all possible, however, I feel it is just as good to get an appetite for natural, relaxed breathing. This is something you can live with all day, without having to do it as an exercise.

How the Breath Tenses Up

There is much more to the breath than a simple in and out. When things go wrong, the breath gets locked or jerky or constricted, or becomes too deep or too shallow or too fast. There are infinite gradations between the stopped breath of shock and the loose spontaneous breathing of sleep.

Each kind of breathing (and non-breathing) is appropriate in certain circumstances. Our nervous systems are designed for a range of situations, and the breath reflects this. Let me explain how the tension-relaxation cycle is mirrored by the breath.

We are designed to freeze when we feel there is imminent danger. A gazelle, for example, will stand stock still if it suspects a lioness is near. It will hold its breath, partly because breathing is noisy and it needs to listen carefully for the slightest sound.

Ideally the freeze lasts only a few seconds. If the danger is real, the animal will quickly finish eating what is in its mouth. It often defecates and urinates as well (just as people often want to go to the toilet when anxious) to lighten the load if it has to start running.

The gazelle now moves into an arousal stage with rapid shallow breathing (which is a typical symptom of people who suffer panic attacks). This hyperventilation causes more in-breathing than out-breathing and floods the body with the oxygen it needs to metabolize energy quickly.

If the gazelle now flees, her breathing becomes very deep and regular. The explosive alarm response (short rapid breathing) gives way to a sustained energy release over a longer time span.

We often go into bursts of deep breathing when we are faced with demanding situations for several minutes. At such a time, deep steady breathing can give us the energy we need, and help us cope.

Each stage—the freeze, the arousal and the flight—is appropriate to the situation. Unfortunately, we can get stuck in any one of them. Even though the last (deep regular breathing) is obviously better than the first two, we can still overdo it. If you over-oxygenate yourself, you'll burn more energy than you need and feel exhausted afterwards.

How the Breath Relaxes

The above stages are governed by the stress response of the sympathetic nervous system, which revs us up and gets us going. To relax, however, the parasympathetic system comes into play and the breathing changes again.

When the gazelle feels safe, her heavy breathing gives way to panting. In this stage, the out-breath becomes longer than the in-breath. In other words, it is like the hyperventilation of the arousal stage, but in reverse.

Panting is often uncomfortable. When you start to slow down, your attention comes back to yourself and you become aware of the uncomfortable effects of the arousal.

The panting soon gives way to gentle sighs. Sighing is like slow panting, with even longer outbreaths. Since it is quite a relief to leave the high arousal state, sighing soon feels quite enjoyable, signaling your return to homeostasis.

Eventually, you go into natural relaxed breathing. Though this often feels deep and steady, it is significantly different from the regular breathing of the "flight" stage. If you examine it, its pattern is usually not as regular as you might think.

Relaxed, natural breathing can seem rather erratic. It is usually gentle and delicate, with the odd sigh and little "catch-up" breath thrown in. It is highly responsive to whatever emotion is passing through the mind. An angry or happy thought will immediately create ripples in the breath. This is quite natural, the way it should be.

The Space between the Breaths

Finally, when we relax deeply, the breath can stop completely for several seconds at a time. This no-breath occurs at the end of the exhalation. It is the complete opposite of the frozen breath of alarm, which typically occurs at the top of the inhalation.

The emotional tone is also utterly different. When we sigh, we put down all our burdens. A sigh is saying to the mind, "You can take off the armor now. The crisis is over. It's time to rest."

When the mind really hears the message, the result is often a "no-breath." Both body and mind dissolve into that expanding space at the end of the breath. It rarely lasts more than three to four seconds, but it can seem like forever. It is beyond time and space.

When people first notice this space between the breaths, they often say, "I was a bit scared. I wondered if maybe I wasn't breathing enough." In fact, when the mind follows the body into that place of stillness, we hardly need to breathe at all. A still body and mind need very little oxygen to function.

Because this space can feel so lovely, people often try to hold on to it, which unfortunately destroys it. The no-breath occurs only when you let go completely. This also means you let the new in-breath come when it wants to.

Above I have described six phases of the breath. Three relate to tension, control and the sympathetic nervous system. The other three relate to relaxation, letting go of control and the parasympathetic nervous system. They are

1. Freeze—holding the in-breath
2. Arousal—short rapid breath, hyperventilation
3. Flight—deep regular breathing with no gaps
4. Panting/sighing—longer out-breaths than in-breaths
5. Relaxed natural breathing
6. No-breath—the space at the end of the out-breath

Using the Breath to Relax

The breath mirrors the tension/relaxation cycle of the nervous system automatically. However, we can also use it as a kind of steering wheel to help us relax consciously. Like Chairman Mao, it is the Master Helmsman. I will talk about how to release the breath casually during the day, then I'll describe a formal breath meditation.

You may be in a meeting or about to give a presentation. If you notice the breath is short and jerky, this indicates that the body is in panic or high arousal mode. So the solution is obvious. You move forward from the arousal to the flight stage: deep, regular, controlled breathing. This breaks the lock, and gives you the oxygen and energy you need to function well.

Deep regular breathing, however, is still an aroused state under the control of the sympathetic nervous system. If you want to move into the relaxing phase, you need to let the deep breathing go.

The simplest way to initiate the relaxation response is to sigh. After two or three deep controlled breaths, you let the breath go. When you sigh, the out-breath becomes considerably longer than the in-breath.

At first, the sighs feel a little forced and controlled. They may pass through a slightly uncomfortable "panting" stage before becoming smoother. The sigh signifies a shift from the active, fix-it mindstate that goes with tension to the "let it all go" mindstate of relaxation. There can be some emotional discomfort with this: sadness or awareness of fatigue, for example.

A few deep sighs is enough. Then the sighs become lighter, less controlled, slower and smoother, and less like a full-bodied sigh. It may be better to think "short in-breaths and longer out-breaths." This is a transitional stage, leading to natural, relaxed breathing that involves "just watching" the breath, with as little control as possible. No anxiety or effort. Just letting the breath do what it wants to do.

Sometimes deep regular breathing is called for. At other times, a few sighs leading to natural relaxed breathing are the solution. A minute or two here or there during the day is quite enough to keep the tension from building to the bursting point.

Formally Meditating on the Breath

When we focus on the breath, we eventually evoke the quality of relaxed, natural breathing. When we relax fully, we feel safe and at ease in our bodies, like a baby in its mother's arms.

This quality of breath is like the gentle waves and swells of a tranquil ocean. The movement of the water is rhythmic and natural, and yet no two waves are exactly alike. For this reason, we don't try to make the breathing regular. It can obstruct the natural irregularities.

When we relax, we trust that the body and mind can find their own equilibrium. We let the body breathe as it wishes. Nonetheless, it is not easy to "just watch" the breath without subtly influencing it. There is a feedback loop between body and mind. As the mind becomes more clear and still, it has a causal effect on the breath, which becomes more gentle and tranquil. Similarly, the ebb and flow of the breath can have a soothing, almost hypnotic, effect on the mind, like watching the waves at the beach.

Many people can't watch the breath without controlling it. This is okay, so long as the control is minimal and sympathetic. In practice, this means you smooth off the rough edges of the breath, but you definitely don't try to breathe deeply or "correctly."

Some people find that watching the breath actually increases their anxiety. Despite themselves, they are afraid they are not breathing right and feel they have to take control of it. Such people may find that the body itself, which is less controllable, is a better meditation object than the breath.

❋

The Breath Meditation

Sit down and let your body settle. Do a quick scan if you wish. Sigh a couple of times to break the lock in the breathing.

Notice where in the body you feel the breathing most clearly. It could be in the belly, or the chest, or the throat or in the nostrils. Let the mind settle in there, and bring the detail of the breath into focus.

Watch the breath rise and fall, or the body expand and contract. Include other sensations such as the heartbeat if you feel it, or feelings of tension or pain.

To stay on track it can be helpful to count the breaths. It's good to double-count. You say "one" on the in-breath and "one" on the out-breath. Then "two" on the next in-breath and "two" on the next out-breath. You continue counting up to 4 or 8 or 10 repeatedly.

If the mind gets distracted you just return to the count. Alternatively, you could "name the distraction" and give it a place in the corner of your mind. So you say "traffic" or "headache" or "work," if you find yourself thinking about any of these, and then return to the count.

BASIC INSTRUCTIONS

1. Sit and let the body settle
2. Feel yourself breathing and count the breaths
3. Let other thoughts and sensations pass in the background—just watching
4. Enjoy the feeling of the body relaxing

❀

NINE

Acute Pain

❀

Physical or emotional pain is inevitable much of the time, but we don't need to let it stress us out. Hoping to always avoid it is like hoping it will never rain, and that every day will be sunny. We have to find some way of being comfortable with the pain that goes with being alive.

This situation became very clear to me two years ago. At night, on a lonely country road, I came across a head-on collision between an old sedan and a small truck. "Get me out of here," said the driver of the sedan. She had a broken foot and a broken arm. Her elderly passenger and I pulled her out of the wreckage and tried to make her comfortable on the shoulder, while waiting a full thirty minutes for the ambulance.

The driver in the truck was in much worse shape. It took ninety minutes to cut him free of the wreckage. And he said exactly the same thing as the woman: "Get me out of here!"

What they both meant was, "Get me away from this pain!" This is the terrible thing about pain. Sometimes we can't escape it at all. For those two, their pain went with them in the emergency helicopter.

The male driver was better prepared for pain. He was so drunk he barely knew what was happening. This is our usual strategy with pain. Most of our lives we try to avoid or ignore it. But sometimes it ruthlessly hunts us down and there is no place to hide.

Some of my best students are those with chronic pain. They are particularly motivated. They often say meditation is the only thing that works. Sometimes the pain vanishes completely. More commonly, the pain remains but becomes manageable. In either scenario, they manage to relax and be mentally comfortable in the midst of pain.

If we know how to work with the big pain, we also know how to cope with the scores of smaller daily pains. If we consistently overreact, we are in trouble. If, however, we "feel the pain and do it anyway," we can be relaxed and happy, even if things are not going our way. Pain doesn't need to destroy our enjoyment of life or be an obstacle to physical relaxation.

Pain Is Part Physical, Part Mental

We expect pain to be in proportion to the degree of physical injury. However, pain specialists know this is rarely the case. One person with back pain can be in agony with imperceptible physical damage. Another feels almost nothing despite major physical trauma.

Certain cultures, races and classes of people feel pain quite differently from others. Cultures shape our personal perception of pain. Some people endure physical injury stoically and actually feel little pain. Others are socially encouraged to be hypersensitive and coddle every pinprick.

Pain can be hypnotized away. A child with a scratched knee runs to mother, and the mother can literally "kiss it better." The pain shrinks from extreme to mild and soon vanishes. Most of us know how a pain seems extreme when we are tense, and diminishes when we relax.

Pain is psychosomatic. Our reactions to the physical sensation can amplify our actual perception of pain four-fold. While pain seems to be purely physical, it may in fact be one part sensation and four parts emotional amplification.

Pain is a cry for help and a warning. The body screams, "Help me! Drop everything else! Something horrible is happening and it feels dangerous!" Fear, anger and adrenaline flood through the system and we respond.

Yet even when we know what is happening, we still sense the pain through the filter of our fear and anger. Our back hurts. We know it won't kill us, but we respond as if it will. We rail at the injustice of life. We curse our own stupidity in letting it happen.

We are afraid it may get worse. We are reminded, against all our wishes and hopes, that human bodies are almost defenseless against pain, sickness, aging and death. We project all those unresolvable emotions onto a slight tear in the lower back. No wonder it hurts!

Let the Pain Speak

When aware of pain, we have three possible strategies: we can ignore it, fight it or "just watch" it. Ignoring pain works well for minor things. If we nick our finger or stub our toe, we swear, grit our teeth and get on with it. In other words, we acknowledge it and assess the damage, but don't dwell on it. But if a middle-aged jogger pushes through the pain barrier in his knees, serious damage can be done.

Alternatively, we can regard the pain with considerable hatred and go to battle with it. We try to "get rid of it" and tense the body around it, confining it in a prison of tight muscles. This is usually counterproductive, driving the pain underground and making it fester. (More on this in the next chapter.)

By now, the two strategies mentioned above should seem rather familiar: they are merely subtle forms of the fight-or-flight response. It is as if we see pain as an alien army on the border and feel we have no options but to attack it or escape it.

However, as we know from international politics, another way to solve disputes is negotiation. Meditation allows us to cool down enough to sit at a table with the pain and listen to it. The results are often wonderful. We may find the pain is not the demon we thought it was—our response was making the situation worse.

Meditation doesn't smother the pain. It changes our response to it. If we drop our rage and fear and "just watch" the pain, with detachment, it becomes a purely physical sensation. We may realize, to our embarrassment, it is more manageable than we thought it was.

When we consciously relax into the pain, it often fades from extreme to something tolerable. If we relax to the point of sleep, it may cease to be painful at all. In the "body asleep, mind awake" state common to much meditation, we lose our habitual identification with the body. The pain now just becomes pure sensation that doesn't upset us in any way.

Meditating on pain is like kissing frogs. When you accept it, it changes. If we cease hostilities towards it, it can relax and free itself up. It may be difficult to treat it with care and affection, as we would a sick child, but we can at least give it space to be present. When we negotiate a peace with the enemy, we may find we can live with him after all.

Paradoxically, pain can be a marvelous object to meditate on. It is often more fascinating than the breath or a mantra, so you are less distracted by other things. Relaxation comes when you focus well on anything, whether it is pleasant or not. Pain can easily relax you to the point of sleep, as one of my students found in class.

She was in such pain she could not even sit in a chair. She did her meditations lying down, or propped up against the wall with a cushion. She was desperate to learn the pain meditation.

When we did the meditation, however, she was terribly disappointed. She relaxed so deeply in the first two minutes that she went to sleep. She no longer heard my instructions, so she couldn't remember what to do!

✸

Pain Meditation

The essence of this meditation is acceptance. If you have a hidden agenda to get rid of the pain, this hostile approach will keep you from relaxing. Remember that the pain is not an invader: it is part of you.

First relax the body and mind as usual. Then turn to the pain. It can be colossal capital "P" pain or just a mild discomfort.

Sense it exactly. With detachment, like a surveyor, map out its boundaries. Slowly and deliberately, trace its outline with your mind. Notice how deep or shallow it is. If you want, you can picture it as a color or texture or as an object.

Relax into it, using the breath. When noticing pain we tend to hold our breath, as if to pull away from it. Now let the breath be loose and free. When you breathe out, feel you are sliding down the breath into the pain.

Caress the pain with the breath. Seek out the very epicenter, where the pain is most intense, or where it seems to come from. Let go all your emotional resistance to it.

Notice that the pain is not solid. It consists of vibrations—throbbing, aching, pulsing, shooting or whatever. Encourage the pain to move in whatever way it wants. Give it space to move freely. Let your body be soft around it.

Watch the free play of the pain with curiosity and interest. The pain may get worse, then diminish, and then appear elsewhere. If one pain subsides, go to another and repeat the process: map out the boundaries, find the epicenter, relax into it using the breath, be soft around the pain and watch it play. Don't skim across the surface. Let the pain emerge in all its detail.

Check that the body as a whole is actually relaxing. Even a good pain meditation can be a little intense. It is usually best to finish by letting the pain go and doing some other meditation for the last minute or so. For further options, see the meditation on the negatives in Chapter 21.

CORE INSTRUCTIONS

Sense the outlines of the pain
Relax into the center of it, using the breath
Let the pain express itself fully
Relax your body around the pain
Finish by meditating on the breath

✸

TEN

Migraines and Chronic Pain

✸

Meditating to Defuse a Migraine

People who take up meditation to cope with migraines are often very happy with the results. For some of them, meditation can be an instant cure. Years ago, a bank manager came to my courses. He had suffered migraines every week for decades but from the very first class, they stopped. He attended two whole courses to make sure. I still see him from time to time. "Still no migraines," he says, "unless I stop meditating for a while."

Migraines and headaches are often a dysfunctional release of tension. Like people with hypertension, migraine sufferers often have high levels of pervasive muscular tension. Instead of tensing and relaxing within a normal range, they tense up to an extreme degree. The release then comes explosively.

Meditation helps this situation by keeping the pervasive body tension below the point that triggers off a migraine. This is what the bank manager was doing. By lowering his overall tension just 10%, he kept himself below the threshold.

In the early stages of a migraine, chronically tight neck and shoulder muscles constrict the carotid artery and impede the flow of blood to the head. Generally, you have already been in "fight" response for hours by being tense, mentally active and blocking the unpleasant sensations that are mounting within you. Of course, this amplifies the problem.

The full flush of the migraine or headache actually occurs as you relax, or when you can't hold onto that muscle tension any longer. This allows a rush of blood to the head, swelling the blood vessels and making them ache and throb.

If you intervene at an early stage, you can turn the process around. Instead of an uncontrollable explosion, you can release the rising tension gracefully, like taking the lid off a pressure cooker. When one of my students feels a migraine coming on, she invites it forth. She says, "Come on! Do your worst!" Instead of running away from it, she sends her mind into every ache, pulsation and twinge and welcomes it. This gives her a reassuring sense of being in control, even in situations where the drugs fail to help her. Even more importantly, she is shifting her emotional attitude. She is abandoning the suppressed anger and fear that amplify the problem.

To prevent migraines and headaches, the best meditations are breath and body-based practices. It is difficult to focus on anything else when the sensations are so unpleasant. So you make the best of a bad situation and make the pain your meditation object.

The Causes of Chronic or Recurrent Pain

We like to think of pain as being purely physical. We would much rather attribute our pain to a crumbling joint or torn muscle than admit that our mental attitude has something to do with it. So we try to treat it with drugs, surgery and other medical interventions—usually with indifferent success.

Since pain is definitely not "all in the mind," let us look at the physiology first. The perception of pain is designed to protect the body. Pain sensations tell us when certain tissues are in danger and enable us to respond. Any torn muscle or piece of burnt skin will send a signal to the brain. It is what happens after this that interests us here.

Yes, it hurts. But how much it hurts and how you respond depend on your current emotional state. If you feel vulnerable, anxious and depressed, it will hurt a lot. If you are clear-minded and can assess it rationally, it may not hurt much at all. If you react with anger and frustration, you activate the whole sympathetic nervous system response, which will generally amplify the body's discomfort. If you are relaxed about the pain, you feel a little blip and the body returns to homeostasis.

So, does the mind cause pain? Not quite. One pain researcher puts it this way: "Psychological factors rarely cause pain; but the longer chronic pain exists, the more likely it is that emotional factors are prolonging it."[1] Here are some of the ways pain can be aggravated by emotional stress.

If we are nursing a pain or injury, we can be reluctant to move much at all. We take it easy, do no exercise and consequently lose muscle tone. We are also inclined to favor our weakness, which puts more stress on other muscles. With back pain, this often means our posture becomes distorted, leading to further problems.

If anxiety is making us tense, our metabolic rate rises. We may be burning a considerable amount of energy while apparently doing nothing. The original pain is now amplified by strain and fatigue.

The stress response cuts down the blood supply to certain parts of the body—particularly the digestive system, the sexual organs and the skin. But tension itself produces bad circulation, particularly in the areas of maximum tension. If tight muscles, say in the neck or scalp or thighs, stay chronically tight, they can lock into spasm.

Tight muscles get starved of oxygen and, just like us if we were being suffocated, they soon start to make a fuss. They do it by sending pain signals to the brain, forcing us to do something. So if you are chronically anxious, the stress response stirs up a wide range of painful feeling throughout your body. In other words, oxygen starvation may be the basic cause of dull chronic pain.[2]

John Sarno, author of *The Bodymind Prescription,* argues that the causality behind unnecessary pain goes something like this: Repressed emotions, particularly anger, trigger the sympathetic nervous response. This reduces blood circulation in certain parts of the body, leading to mild oxygen deprivation. This registers as pain, numbness, tingling, weakness, aching, etc. This is the emotion—oxygen starvation—pain sequence.

Sarno also argues that we often exaggerate pain to avoid looking at the underlying feeling. It feels safer to grimace in physical pain than to allow broad-spectrum rage at the world to erupt. Pain is a way of locking up feelings and making sure they stay out of the picture.

People who push this to the extreme are called "somatizers." They are nightmares for doctors, and a major drain on the health system. Such people seem to have heart problems or back pain or chronic fatigue or irritable bowel or hypoglycemia or almost anything else. In fact, their presenting symptoms are manifestations of unacknowledged emotional conflicts that can't be helped medically. This does not stop them from demanding useless treatments and operations.

It may take years to persuade such people to seek psychological help, but if they do, their prognosis often changes dramatically. As one psychologist puts it, "It is a characteristic of human beings that we prefer physical pain to a psychic pain that seems inescapable. The goal of psychotherapy is to find alternatives to translating stress into a physical symptom and eventually to resolve the emotional problem that led to it."[3]

Disarming the Emotional Causes of Pain

If the above is even partly true, it explains why psychological approaches to pain, including therapy, stress management and meditation, can have such excellent results.

Common to all of these approaches is one factor: they allow the sufferer to look at pain with some rationality and detachment. This alone may be the reason they work. They enable the patient to temporarily put aside the usual fear, anger or denial about the pain. As the emotional heat diminishes, the pain often does too.

At the Stress Reduction Clinic of the University of Massachusetts, Jon Kabat-Zinn teaches a Buddhist "mindfulness" practice that particularly works on this simple recognition of pain. Rather than focusing directly on one thing, the meditators simply watch dispassionately whatever thoughts, feelings and sensations are passing through their consciousness at the moment.

Inevitably, a pain sufferer starts to realize how his emotional reactions intensify the pain, and how he has another choice—to simply watch and accept—that reduces it. By reducing the anxiety, depression and hostility that usually accompany pain, the Stress Reduction Clinic has had extraordinary success rates over the years.[4]

The Effects of Enhanced Sensing

While psychotherapy helps people by giving them a verbal awareness of their pain, meditation has a more physical and immediate effect. As I described in the early chapters, meditation shifts the mind from thinking mode to sensing mode. Within seconds of starting to meditate, for example, sounds may suddenly seem louder. People are more aware of traffic, birds, a ticking clock, a machine whirring or a distant conversation.

When they were verbally active—thinking, talking or listening—their sensing function was eclipsed, and they literally didn't hear the sounds around them. As soon as they shift into sensing mode, however, it is as if the volume has been turned up. I ask my students to use this as a sign that they are starting to relax.

This enhanced sensing also applies to their bodies. As the endorphins of the stress response fade away, the hidden aches and pains and latent fatigue in the body are likely to surface. Once again, I tell them this is an excellent sign that they have activated the relaxation response.

Some people, however, find the physical sensations of relaxation distinctly uncomfortable, and those in pain become more aware of the pain as they relax. Occasionally someone will report, "That meditation was horrible! I couldn't settle and I was aching all over and my headache got worse." They may also add, "I just feel too bad to meditate today. I just can't do it. I won't stay for the rest of the class. If you'll excuse me, I'll go home now."

One woman asked, "Why is this happening? I thought meditation was supposed to make you feel good." When I suggested she was
just recognizing exactly how bad she felt, she burst into tears on the
spot. Since I have seen this process many times now, I persuaded her
to stay in the room for the next meditation. "I can guarantee it will feel
much better," I promised, and it did. She gave me a big smile when she
left the class.

I usually do two or three meditations each class. People often find
an uncomfortable first meditation flushes the pain to the surface, and
the benefits of this become obvious in the second.

If you are very stressed, many of the physiological changes that
accompany relaxation are potentially uncomfortable. As endorphin
levels fade, numb muscles regaining sensation are often painful. The
increased blood flow to the skin can produce an itchy feeling. A reac-
tivated digestive system can initially feel nauseous. Relaxed neck muscles can allow an increased flow of blood to the head, swelling blood
vessels into a mild headache. Tight muscles can release in awkward
twitches or spasms.

In other words, if you are very stressed, nausea, headaches, itch-
ing, muscle pain and twitching may well accompany the relaxation
process for you. If you don't like it, you have the option: you can simply tense up again, have some coffee, start talking, watch TV, and the
symptoms are quite easy to suppress—temporarily.

Meditating to Defuse Emotion

The relaxation response also loosens up emotional tightness. As you
relax into your body, just as it is, you notice your underlying mood,
whether you like it or not. It's not just your body that is stressed and
tired—your mind could be grumpy, restless, upset or irritable as well.

Any pain inevitably mirrors, or holds within it, a little bundle of
emotion. But because meditating is a passive state, you become able
to "just watch" your anger, sadness or fear, without having to change
them. When you accept their presence, they usually pass fairly rapidly.

One of my older and more respectable students said, "I love meditation because it is one time in my life that I don't have to be bright and
cheerful."

It is good to remember that the original cause of all stress is emotion. Something makes us sad or angry or fearful and the hypothalamus
initiates the sympathetic nervous system response from that point.
Knowing this, we can actually use physical pain as a way of disarming
emotion.

So, instead of trying to feel good, you could let yourself feel bad
instead. Instead of focusing on the breath, you can go straight to the
discomforts. You can focus in turn on a headache, a sore stomach, an
itchy skin or a sense of exhaustion. By dropping your resistance to
each pain and allowing it to come forth, you can quickly reduce your
pervasive irritability. Generally you will relax rapidly, even if some of
the pain continues to hang around.

✳

Awareness, or "Watching the Stream"

Most meditations emphasize focusing on an object to detach you from
the peripheral thoughts and feelings. This practice enables you to
include things in the meditation that would otherwise be distractions.

In this practice, you imagine the mind like a stream of consciousness, with the various thoughts, sensations, images and feelings as
objects floating by. And you just watch them come and go.

To keep from being sucked into the stream, you stay anchored on
the bank by holding onto a standard meditation object such as the
breath. In other words, the breath is the seat from which you watch the
stream.

So the meditation starts in the usual way. You settle the body and
bring the breath into focus. When you feel yourself relaxing, you
expand your awareness. Without actively looking for anything, you
notice what else is in consciousness at that moment.

It could be pain, a noise outside, a sense of sadness or fatigue, an itch, a thought of last night's TV. Notice it dispassionately and with acceptance. Notice how it all passes sooner or later and then something else emerges.

Every few seconds, "name" whatever is in consciousness at that time. You could name sensations ("pain ... traffic ...") or the content of thoughts ("food ... David ... work ...") or emotions ("bored ... angry ..."). This nonjudgmental awareness keeps you in observer mode.

Just name the most obvious things. If you tried to name everything, you would be very busy. In this way, anything that would normally be a distraction becomes part of the meditation. Refrain from getting interested in what you notice. That will suck you into the stream.

Don't lose contact with the breath. Stay on your seat. Ideally, you focus on the breath half the time and watch the flow half the time. This meditation is cultivating a bland, clear mirror-like mind that doesn't automatically pursue good thoughts and fight off bad ones.

This practice—just watching and naming the passing thoughts and sensations—inevitably leads to small insights. After all, you are actually observing how your mind reacts. You are likely to see how you can't control what comes into the mind, but you can choose how you react to it. If your reaction is neutral, you relax and the mind stays clear. If you get engaged, you tense up. It's your choice.

CORE INSTRUCTIONS
1. Focus on a meditation object as usual
2. When you feel settled, dispassionately notice what else is in the mind
3. Every few seconds, "name" what is dominant, whether it seems important or not
4. Alternate your attention between the breath and the "stream"

❀

ELEVEN

Insomnia and Fatigue

❀

Relaxation is the art of turning on the relaxation response, which is the branch of the nervous system that takes you down towards sleep. Consequently, meditation is excellent for people suffering insomnia.

While the instinct to sleep at night and take it easy during the day is as natural as eating or breathing, some people lose it completely. They have to come to meditation classes to re-learn how to sleep!

About a third of people coming to my courses have trouble sleeping. Some have trouble going to sleep. Some fall asleep quickly but wake too early. Others just sleep badly, half thinking and half snoozing through the night. By the end of the courses, about half are sleeping better, some very much better.

Often the results are immediate. Many people say they have their best sleep of the week on the night they come to their meditation class. In other words, just to meditate deeply once a week has immediate benefits.

Meditation helps insomniacs in several ways. It initiates the sleep response before going to bed. It defuses the thinking that tends to keep the person awake. It helps them go back to sleep if they wake in the small hours. And if they remain awake at night, it enables them to relax in that state instead of fretting.

Insomniacs tend to be chronic thinkers. As soon as they stop "doing," they start "thinking." When they go to bed, all the unfinished thoughts of the day crowd in on them. "At last!" says the brain. "A chance to think without distraction."

Unfortunately, the luxury of thinking is incompatible with sleep. The emotional charge behind the thoughts keeps you stirred up. Nonetheless, after an hour or so you do fall asleep, out of exhaustion if nothing else, and the thoughts are put on hold.

Not for long, however. Insomniacs are often addicted to thinking. Consequently, the thoughts are just waiting for a chance to leap to the surface again. The body rests for three or four hours, and gets a little energy back: just enough to wake up and start thinking again.

Meditating before Going to Bed

Many people try to combat thoughts by making their minds blank. Blankness, however, is not an easy state to hold. Even if you do achieve a temporary emptiness, the thoughts will soon crowd back.

Meditation works quite differently. You divert your mind from thinking to sensing. This is the guaranteed route of escape. When you focus fully on the breath or sounds or a mantra, the mind detaches from the thoughts that were keeping you awake. If you are tired and also lying down, you are certain to fall asleep.

Meditation is good preparation for sleep, as long as you don't meditate too long. If you do a long sitting meditation before you go to bed, this can actually refresh you and paradoxically make it harder to fall asleep.

Generally, a longish meditation has three phases. In the first, the mind is quite active and you don't seem to be relaxing much. In the second, you break free of the inner dialogue and start to relax so rapidly you can drop close to sleep within a minute or so. You feel the mind becoming vague and dreamy.

If you continue, however, the body rests and the mind wakes up again. This is the third stage, where you have the combination of relaxed body and alert mind. This is the ideal for a formal meditation.

If you meditate before going to bed, make sure you don't go through to stage three. Meditate just to extract yourself from thinking.

Five or ten minutes is usually more than enough. When you notice the first signs that the body is relaxing—heaviness, nodding, loose breathing—stop meditating and go to bed. Catch that downward slide into sleep.

Meditating while in Bed

You can also meditate in bed to put yourself to sleep. Now the situation changes. Once you have been in bed a few minutes, your thoughts tend to be vague and rambly but they can still keep you awake. Paradoxically, the way to go to sleep when you are in bed is to focus intently.

So you pay good attention to your meditation object and don't indulge the background thoughts. Get the mind as clear and focused as you can. Only this will distance you from the thoughts that are keeping you awake. You can't waffle your way back to sleep. The progression usually goes: muddy mind—clear mind—sleep.

Many of my students report that meditation is wonderful for putting themselves back to sleep. "I just focus on a few breaths and I'm gone." Even if this fails, meditation can be very useful.

If we lie awake and think, we burn a lot of energy and get up in the morning exhausted. If we are still unable to sleep but we meditate through the small hours instead of worrying, we will conserve energy. The body still rests, the mind becomes clearer and we are more likely to dip in and out of sleep.

Whether we are kept awake by pain or emotional turmoil or a partner's snoring, it can be invaluable to meditate. You may not actually go to sleep, but the mind becomes more detached and dispassionate. You may not like the situation, but you don't have to overreact.

While not perfect, this can be vastly preferable to rising in the morning irritated and exhausted. One of my students was in such pain he rarely slept for more than half an hour at a time. He found that although he remained awake much of the night, by meditating in the small hours, he rested far more deeply than he had for years.

When meditating in bed, any meditation practice will do. It is usually best, however, to be lying on your back. If you curl up on your side the mind rarely stays focused.

A good strategy, if your partner agrees, is to meditate on music. A CD player with a remote control is ideal. CDs don't stop with a noisy click the way tapes do, and a remote control means you can switch it on if you wake in the night, without having to get up and fuss around.

When meditating in bed, go for a sharp clear mind to distance you from other thoughts. When listening to music, for example, try to hear as much detail as you can. If you are lying down and physically tired anyway, you are bound to fall asleep.

The Effects of Chronic Fatigue

The state of perpetual arousal is exhausting. A worrier, just sitting in a room all day, will burn more energy than a bricklayer who is enjoying his work. His nervous system is sending electrical impulses to most of the muscles in his body, causing them to contract and stay contracted. Since muscles make up 40% of our body weight, Thomas Leaman, in *Healing the Anxiety Disorders*, says, "All this activity, the contraction of these microscopic fibers, has used an enormous amount of energy, even though we have not moved at all. This leaves individual muscles exhausted and in a state of severe fatigue."[1]

This is a state of internal conflict. The flexors are pulling against the extensors. The body is in readiness for fight-or-flight, and yet stays immobile for hours. "When the muscle tension becomes generalized all over the body, the symptoms disperse and the person starts complaining of aching all over."

I imagine that at least 20% of us feel "chronically fatigued" much of our adult lives. It is an unacknowledged epidemic which, like muscular tension, is so common that it is regarded as normal. How many adults do we meet who have an abundance of energy? Very few.

Fatigue is both a sign of sickness and a contributing cause. It is a huge contributor to the rate of wear and tear in the body. Some people literally die of exhaustion—too burnt-out to keep going. Their bodies may sink from hyper-arousal to fatigue in an attempt to restore home-ostasis, but they are just too tired to bounce back.

Fatigue also leads to emotional sickness. It's easy to feel good when our energy is up. It takes more maturity to enjoy the times when our energy is down. While the "down" states are perfectly natural, and good for rest and reflection, many people are afraid of them. The down times make them feel depressed, frustrated and unable to cope. They often turn to food or alcohol, and feel resentful towards their workload or other people—just because their energy is low.

The identity of people suffering from the illness called Chronic Fatigue Syndrome often revolves around burning lots of energy. They tend to be lively, intelligent, high achievers who epitomize the poet Blake's dictum, "Energy is eternal delight."

Unfortunately, they rarely notice when their bodies and minds need to rest. When Chronic Fatigue Syndrome kicks in, they often plunge into mindstates that are completely alien to them. Exhaustion, inactivity, helplessness and despair can overwhelm them and lead to a painful re-evaluation of who they actually are. Frequently, their whole lifestyle and self-image have to change.

Paying off the Sleep Debt

One centenarian, when asked the perennial question "What has con-tributed to your long life?" replied, "I always got plenty of sleep." Simi-larly, a Zen master, when asked the secret of his attainment, said, "When hungry, I eat. When tired, I sleep." Obviously, one of the little-known secrets of wise old men is to get enough sleep.

Years ago I had the chance to discover a healthy pattern of sleep-ing and resting. I did a seven-month retreat and, like a cat, I let myself sleep whenever I wanted.

By the end, I was sleeping five or six times a day, often for only fifteen minutes at a time. It was glorious! It felt so natural, and yet so alien to our Western culture. It seems likely that if we could only listen to our inner clock, and sleep and rest when we needed to, many of our health problems would vanish.

The body/mind tenses and relaxes regularly during the day. We rev up and slow down roughly on a 90-minute cycle. We have these epicycles of arousal and rest within the usual 24-hour cycle of being awake during the day and asleep at night.

Unfortunately, we tend to stubbornly fight these natural cycles. We try to stay revved up for 16 hours and get all our rest at night. We try to power through the low patches in the day and grimly hang on to the highs.

However, if we don't pace ourselves well during the day, we don't sleep well at night. We need the little rests during the day, when we just "take it easy," in order to fully benefit from the big rest at night. Otherwise we take too much unfinished business to bed with us. If you can reduce the daytime charge by 10 to 20%, you will find the thoughts don't have as compulsive a grip on you when you try to fall asleep.

If we don't get enough sleep, or enough relaxed time during the day, we build up a "sleep debt." You can see this most clearly by the way people sleep in on Saturday or Sunday mornings, trying to catch up on the sleep they lost during the week.

Decades of inadequate sleep and rest have consequences as serious as habitually overspending the budget. Just as the overspent pennies soon turn into dollars, so the sleep debt can inexorably grow into physical and emotional bankruptcy.

When people go on a retreat, they often discover how big their sleep debt actually is. They try to meditate religiously, but their bodies will grab any opportunity to crash. As a rule of thumb, I say that the sleep debt is being paid off during the first third of any retreat, however long it is. The retreatants commonly feel sleepy for days and come to realize how exhausted they actually are. Sometimes they say things like, "I didn't realize how tired I was. I think I've been this tired for years."

The sleep debt often builds to a critical mass by the time people are in their forties. They lose their passion for work and family, and each day becomes a meaningless grind. This is when the need for a complete break, or a very long holiday, or a sabbatical, becomes crucial for our health and mental well-being.

However, just getting away for a month or a year may still not be enough. Sleeping a lot and taking it easy may not really change the ingrained emotional habits that caused the fatigue in the first place. People who are bedridden for months, for example, don't necessarily have an abundance of energy as a result.

Sitting in a chair, thinking and worrying, can literally burn more calories than during physical activity. You may be much more at ease, in body and mind, working in the garden. This is why people who take time off "to think things through" don't necessarily come back refreshed.

Habitual fatigue is an unacknowledged epidemic. The solutions, therefore, are not that clear. It is not just a matter of sleeping more. It often means changing values and lifestyles, and this may feel as if it's going against the grain of twenty-first century culture.

The Little Sleeps

To overcome fatigue, we obviously need to sleep better. However, we are unlikely to sleep well unless we can also relax occasionally during the day. Most of us have little inadvertent strategies to help us do this. We take tea-breaks; we sit and read the paper mindlessly; we zone out in meetings or while driving; we find ourselves "going slow" for a few minutes after lunch; we putter around the house doing nothing much, or we take the dog for a walk.

These are "little sleeps," when the metabolic rate drops somewhat and we collect our energy. We take a few steps in the direction of sleep without going the whole way. Without these little rests, our day would be intolerably stressed.

Once you learn to meditate, you realize how valuable these little breaks are and you get more out of them. You notice how many opportunities you have to slow down for a few seconds or minutes during the day, and you become skilled at taking time out.

One friend was meditating during a long meeting. Afterwards, a colleague said to him, "Your eyes were open, you had an intelligent expression on your face. But you weren't really there, were you?" He needed a little more practice. In time, no one would notice.

Meditation is about pacing yourself. To be relaxed during the day, we learn to use the right amount of energy for the task at hand—neither too much nor too little. When we talk to a difficult person, we say just what is necessary and no more. If we need a rest from conversation, we put our usual thoughts on hold and consciously taste the coffee.

It may be tempting when we relax to just let the mind wander and free-associate. However, it's much more efficient to consciously focus on something. When the mind wanders we are still indulging the thoughts. When we focus, we leave them behind.

Resting the Mind through Activity

Many people relax deeply and get their minds clear while running or swimming. If you are engrossed in the gardening, enjoying what you do and see, you are bound to feel refreshed afterwards.

This morning I read the comments of a golfer who eventually won the current championship. "Everyone should have a psychologist," he said. (His girlfriend is one, and she was advising him.) He has a little routine before each shot that includes focusing on the breath and counting to five to clear his thoughts.

"It's just about keeping relaxed on the golf course and finding out whether I'm under-aroused or over-aroused. It's about keeping that midstream where peak performance is."

I have now helped several athletes and performers improve by teaching them how to pace themselves. One singer felt her energy tended to peak too early so that she was already tired before she went on stage. By learning to relax as necessary and rev herself up as necessary, she won a national singing competition and went on to an international career.

For most of us, our situation is more mundane, but no less critical to our health. If we habitually overreact, day after day, year after year, we burn up the fuel supplies and feel old before our time. And if we underreact because of exhaustion and lack of enthusiasm, we don't perform well and our life goes to the dogs.

Many people relax best through activity. It's often counterproductive to sit still in a quiet place to relax. Some people in that situation simply sit and worry instead. For such people, contemplating their navels can be far more exhausting than physical work, leading to despair and self-pity rather than to relaxation.

While we do need to rest, we can't overcome habitual fatigue by only doing less. Paradoxically, we actually need to burn energy to get energy. Doing nothing at all, as people who are bedridden often find out, can make you very lethargic and withdrawn. The trick is not to do nothing, but to be relaxed about what you do.

It is not healthy to be sedentary. Our bodies were designed to move a lot each day, as our hunter-gatherer ancestors did. Often we are so locked in our heads that we forget the simple organic pleasure of just walking, just moving, and just using our bodies.

No matter how deeply exhausted we may be, we won't recover unless we are also physically active. Simple activities, like walking a little more each day, are excellent ways to combat fatigue. People who are exhausted usually need less mental activity and more physical activity.

When I lead retreats, I always alternate the sitting meditations with periods of activity such as walking, yoga or swimming. I find that too much sitting meditation makes people more tired. To relax fully, we need to restore the natural epicycles of arousal and relaxation during the day.

❋

Walking Meditations

In some walking meditations, you meditate on the activity of walking itself. In others, you use walking as your posture and meditate on something else. Regardless of what you do, you are bound to relax if you bring your mind into the present and enjoy the sense world. Here are some possibilities.

WALKING COMFORTABLY

When we are tense, we usually walk stiffly. In this meditation, we focus on walking comfortably. So walk normally, but focus inwardly on the sensations of your body.

Enjoy the rhythmic swing of your body. Scan it up and down, using the movement to shake out the tensions you may find. Count the breaths if you want to. Have your eyes a little soft and resting on the ground in front of you, so they don't move around at random.

BREATH MEDITATION WHILE WALKING

Walk comfortably and rhythmically, as in the previous meditation. Feel yourself breathing through your chest, or belly, or hips.

Notice roughly how many steps you take as you breathe in and how many as you breathe out. Usually the out-breath is a little longer than the in-breath. When you find your approximate pattern, synchronize the steps with the breathing, counting the steps. You might count three steps as you breathe in and four as you breathe out. Or your pattern may be five and six, or six and six. Let the pattern change as appropriate, and do this as long as you like.

SNAPSHOT

Anything that brings you into the present, such as counting steps, will heighten your awareness of other sensory input. You could meditate on any of the following, by consciously focusing and pulling the mind back when it wanders.

If something catches your eye while walking, such as a cat, a cloud, a shadow, a flowering plant, take a "snapshot" of it. Intently examine it for a few seconds or a minute, and imprint it in your mind. Play it over in your memory for a few seconds as you walk on. At the end of the day, review your snapshots.

OTHER SENSING MEDITATIONS

You can do a sound or smell meditation. Walk comfortably as usual, but let the mind highlight sounds as they come and go around you. Similarly, you can consciously focus on smells, and whatever associations they may stimulate, while you walk.

You could focus on the wind, coming and going on your skin. This is also a lovely practice to do while sitting outside.

Finally, you could just walk with the intention of staying in the present. In practice this means you consciously focus for a few seconds on whatever sense data catches your mind. You stay with it until something else engages you.

You may go from the sound of your footsteps to the scent of grass to the sound of distant traffic to the sight of children on bikes to the feeling of your breathing. Stay with each for long enough to really enjoy it—at least ten seconds. If you skim too quickly, you will find the mind is likely to entertain thoughts as well.

❀

The Digestive System

❀

We tend to regard our digestive system as being somewhat mechanical and automatic. We stick food in, the useful is extracted from the useless, and life goes on. However, just as we all sleep but don't always sleep well, we all eat but don't always digest well. We have nights of sleeping badly, and we have days of digesting badly.

While we easily make the connection between anxiety and insomnia, we tend to blame bad digestion on other things, such as eating too much of the wrong stuff. Yet the signs are obvious if we look for them. When suddenly alarmed by something, we are often "sick to the stomach." We may feel nauseous and want to vomit or go to the toilet. Our bodies instinctively want to stop digesting and void the food to make us ready for action. All this is classic sympathetic nervous system activity—the stress response acting on our gut.

People who are chronically anxious often suffer persistent problems such as ulcers, heartburn, gas, indigestion, pain, diarrhea and/or constipation. If you get several of these regularly, you can say you have irritable bowel syndrome. While none of these are life-threatening or seem to be precursors to illnesses like bowel cancer, they can certainly wear you down and degrade your quality of life.

The great patriarch of mind/body medicine, Hans Seyle, did his pioneering research on just this subject over fifty years ago. His famous experiments proved that putting rats under stress predisposed them to ulcers, and hundreds of subsequent studies have confirmed this link between stress and the gut.[1] The facts are unarguable, though scientists are still struggling to understand the reasons why. The stress-illness mechanism is not as blatantly obvious with the gut as it is with the cardiovascular system, for example.

For this reason, psychologists have taken a particular interest in the digestive system. The most obvious finding is that poor digestion is a common complaint of chronically anxious people, or those who suffer anxiety disorders. We can broaden this net somewhat to include people who are emotionally vulnerable or just more sensitive than the average Joe. In fact, most of us have trouble digesting food when we are anxious. It is a pretty clear sign that, at that moment at least, we are upset.

How Stress Impacts the Gut

When the body is triggered into fight-or-flight mode, the digestive system switches off. Secretions of saliva and digestive juices dry up. After an initial impulse to defecate or vomit, the muscles in the gut spasm and lock. The shop is closed. Nothing will move until the crisis is felt to have passed.

There is a good reason for this. The process of digestion itself consumes 10 to 20% of the body's available energy. In a perceived crisis, the mind says, "Digestion can wait. We need that energy for action." So it shuts off the process of digestion so that the energy goes instead to the fight-or-flight muscles.

The whole dynamic of arousal and relaxation should occur within a few minutes. Unfortunately, we often sustain high tension for days at a time. Since this is not an environment suited to digestion, we literally have "in-digestion," complete with flatulence, burping, discomfort and an accurate perception that food is sitting heavily in our bellies, going nowhere.

This feeling may be a factor in helping men lose weight. Men, typically, are most obese in their forties and become slimmer thereafter.

Until that age, they can usually eat whatever they like without too much discomfort. After fifty, the pain of overeating forces them to be more moderate.

Our first instinct when stressed is not to eat at all. This is what adrenaline does to us. Some young women find a combination of worry, Diet Coke and cigarettes has the not unwelcome result of keeping them thin.

After the adrenaline rush has passed, however, we commonly have the opposite desire. Glucocorticoids can linger in the bloodstream for hours, giving us an appetite for sweet and fatty foods. So the stress response initially stops appetite but then stimulates it, to replenish our energy supplies.[2] This scenario does not lead to intelligent eating.

If we eat when stressed, we are pushing food into a system that is operating on half-power. Our bodies normally try to store food in our stomachs until we relax enough for digestion to proceed. If we fail to relax, the food gets shoved through eventually, but not very efficiently. Because the sympathetic nervous system inhibits the secretion of digestive juices, the small intestine is less able to absorb nutrients from the food.

Tension has a drastic effect on peristalsis. Ideally, this is a soft rhythmic expansion and contraction of muscles that moves food through the digestive tract. "Muscle fibers can only do two things: contract or relax. During digestion they contract rhythmically, propelling food along its way in an orderly fashion. . . . However, when they respond to danger they only contract, causing the whole tubular system to constrict and the sphincters to shut tightly."[3]

Peristalsis is designed to work in a loose and supple belly. Food should transit from mouth to anus in 12 to 24 hours, which is why we are encouraged to eat plenty of roughage. Constipation and diverticulitis (little bulges in the tract where food gets stuck) are common consequences of inhibited peristaltic activity. A lethargic digestive tract creates the kind of stagnant environment that disease and bacteria thrive in.

In the digestive system, stress rarely causes an illness directly. It usually exacerbates an existing condition or creates the right conditions for it. For example, ulcers are caused by a common bacteria, *Helico-bacter pylori*, but almost all of us comfortably co-exist with this bug. It only gets nasty and starts chewing our duodenum when our stress levels go up.

When we're chronically anxious, our protective stomach lining gets weaker, and hydrochloric acid can actually attack our own bodies. Ulcers seem to form around bits of dead tissue in the lining, which may also be a result of sympathetic nervous system activity. The reduced blood flow to the gut can cause little "infarcts," or micro-deaths, in certain cells, due to lack of oxygen. It is also possible that the anti-inflammatory glucocorticoids, by weakening the immune response, may enable *Helicobacter* to thrive. All in all, stress rarely causes the gut to break down completely, but it can make us very uncomfortable for years.

Meditation Frees Up the Digestive System

The Hunzas are an isolated Himalayan tribe renowned for their long-evity. It is said that their communal mealtimes are always occasions of stress-free conviviality. It is regarded as extremely bad table manners to bring any conflict, external or internal, to the meal. They understand how important it is to eat in a relaxed manner.

Meditation has both an immediate and a long-term effect on the digestive system. A meditator can usually turn on the parasympathetic nervous system in about a minute, though it might take five or ten minutes to relax the body fully.

As you relax, the blood flows back into the digestive system, which then starts to wake up. It is quite common to hear gurgling stomachs in a meditation room—an excellent sign that people are relaxing. Another clear sign is the increase in salivation (when we are tense, the mouth goes dry). One of my students said, "I know I'm relaxing when I have to swallow."

As the musculature and the belly relax, the peristaltic movement of the intestines frees up. If a student has been suffering from constipation, she often finds she wants to go to the toilet after meditation.

If you meditate, you can turn a bad digestion day into a good digestion day.

The long-term benefits are even more valuable. Meditation tunes
us into our bodies and their needs. This means we become smarter
eaters, just because we notice what feels good. Otherwise it might
take us half a century before we really know what food and how much
of it is good for us.

Similarly, if we are less anxious, the neurotic impulse towards
comfort food is weaker. The few extra mouthfuls we eat for comfort
each day can mean the difference, over a decade, between a tolerable
weight and obesity.

People may not realize they have gastrointestinal trouble until
rather late in the day. They often don't start to act until they have irritable bowel syndrome or ulcers or chronic constipation or bowel cancer. Fortunately, the body is quite resilient. I have now seen many people overcome the worst effects of gastrointestinal tract disorders, and
even avoid operations, just by learning to relax and meditate. Stress
reduction programs are frequently included in the medical treatment
of people with irritable bowel syndrome. While most meditations will
have a positive downstream effect on the digestive tract, it is also possible to meditate on it specifically. (For further details see Chapter 20.)

❁

Spot-meditation: Countdown

Have you got 30 seconds to spare? It is amazing how much tension you
can drop in such a short time. This practice can be done anywhere—a
supermarket line, at traffic lights, in a waiting room. All you do is scan
the body with seven deep slow breaths.

INSTRUCTIONS

Wherever you are, free up your posture.
Now let the breath go, enjoying the feeling of release.

Now scan the body over seven breaths, shifting from one stage to the next as you breathe out. You can count from seven to one as you do so:

"Seven":	Breathing through the scalp and forehead
"Six":	Softening the face as you breathe out
"Five":	Breathing through the neck and shoulders, arms and hands
"Four":	Feeling your chest rise and fall
"Three":	Softening in the diaphragm
"Two":	Letting the belly flop out as you breathe
"One":	Breathing through the hips, legs and feet

Finally, let your mind rest anywhere in the body for the time remaining. Or repeat the scan. Notice how your mind has slowed down.

❋

THIRTEEN

Stress and the Immune System

❋

After a fight-or-flight response, the body eventually returns to home-ostasis. Because you have just burned a lot of energy, you are quite ready for a rest.

Your immune system has no such respite. Every minute of the day and night it is in combat with billions of bacteria, viruses, fungi and parasites that would love to colonize your body and raise their progeny. Since this battle starts at birth and finishes with your death, homeosta-sis for the immune system means a manageable level of on-going war.

While most of us know that germs cause diseases, it is less widely known that we are regularly exposed to deadly pathogens without get-ting sick. Most of the time, our immune system is even able to destroy cancer cells or the HIV virus long before they get a foothold.

An immune system (hereafter referred to as IS) in good health can cope with almost anything. Even the bubonic plague killed only a third of the population of Europe, which suggests that two-thirds were probably immune. However, the immune system's war of attrition is exhausting, and as the years go by it functions less and less efficiently.

Young people rarely die of pneumonia, for example, but it's a com-mon terminal illness for the old, or for AIDS sufferers whose immune systems are too depleted to cope. You could say they die not from pneu-monia but from the effects of an exhausted IS.

An abundance of studies have now confirmed what ordinary people have known for a long time. You are more inclined to catch the flu or have a herpes outbreak if you feel stressed, unhappy or depressed.[1] In other words, when your immune system is weak. Usually elevated levels of gluco-corticoids or anti-inflammatory agents in the bloodstream are the culprit.

Similarly, you can say that the state of your IS largely determines how sick or healthy your body is throughout your life. A malfunctioning IS makes the body prone to illness and degenerative disease, and accelerates the aging process.

Three Lines of Defense

The IS is a complex, powerful, high-energy mechanism that is always vigilant against a changing array of possible pathogens. Sometimes the IS mobilizes immense forces for stand-up fights with individual pathogens. The rest of the time it conducts search and destroy missions.

The surfaces of the skin, lungs and the digestive tract form the first line of defense. If any of these surfaces are damaged, by a wound or a lung infection or an ulcer, pathogens can enter the bloodstream.

This is where the second line of defense comes into play. The pathogen is attacked by a complex interaction of macrophages, antibodies, B-cells and T-cells. Many of the signs of illness, such as inflammation, swollen lymph glands, fever and fatigue, are the fire and smoke of the IS at work, rather than the direct effect of the pathogen itself.

If viruses manage to escape the battle in the bloodstream by fleeing into the cells to reproduce, the third line of defense comes into play. Killer T-cells now kill the viruses by a scorched-earth approach. Rather than attacking the viruses directly, they destroy the cells they inhabit. They press the "self-destruct," or suicide, button that is part of the makeup of every cell. In other words, T-cells kill viruses by destroying those of your own cells that they inhabit.

If the Immune System Is Weak

The highly energetic and unpredictable nature of the battle makes the IS vulnerable to malfunction. Its high-energy complexity often gets out of balance. Sometimes the immune system underresponds, and pathogens get through on a regular basis. At other times it overresponds and damages healthy tissue.

A healthy IS will stop a pathogen rapidly at the first or second line of defense. This quick response is common in children who typically will get a high fever (which helps the process of defense), and recover rapidly.

The IS consists of border guards who respond instantly to the invasion and conscripts who can be mobilized as necessary. Since the conscripts often take two or three days to arrive in full force, a pathogen has the advantage of surprise. It can breach the defenses, establish a beachhead and multiply within the first few hours.

If this happens, the body is now facing a serious infection that might take days or weeks to clear. This can stretch the resources of the IS, leaving it relatively weak and unable to respond well to the next invasion.

Often neither the IS nor the pathogen win outright. Instead we live with a degree of persistent low-level hostility that makes us feel not quite sick, but not quite well either. The digestive systems and the respiratory tracts of perfectly healthy people are likely to be in a continuous state of mild inflammation because of their continual exposure to pathogens. This can be regarded as a normal level of warfare.

If the balance tips just slightly the results can be catastrophic. It is common for us to have precancerous cells in the body that the IS routinely destroys. If the IS is stretched thin, however, it may not clean up all of those cells and, once they get a chance, they can multiply very rapidly.

Similarly, if cancers stayed in just one location, they could usually be removed completely by surgery. Unfortunately, they often metastasize and colonize different parts of the body as well.

Cancer cells that break away from the main mass usually get sucked up by the lymphatic system and destroyed in the lymph nodes. If the immune system can't cope, the cancerous cells will both colonize the lymph nodes and re-enter the bloodstream in search of new lands to conquer. When this happens, the indiscriminate firepower of chemotherapy is usually called in to augment the IS.

When the Immune System Overreacts

While a weak IS underlies most illnesses, an overresponsive system can be just as devastating. People can die or suffer disability not from the disease, but from their bodies' overreaction to it.

Usually when the IS meets a pathogen it develops antibodies to this pathogen and remembers the face of the enemy. The next time they meet, the IS responds so rapidly the pathogen can't even get started and we don't get sick at all. This is the principle behind immunization: a small exposure to a weakened pathogen gives us immunity to later exposures to the real thing.

However, the exact opposite can sometimes happen. The body becomes oversensitized by repeated exposure, and responds more excessively each time. I used to work with a beekeeper friend who was often called on to remove wasp nests from near people's homes. Wasps are more aggressive than bees and he was often stung. He finally became so sensitive that with one more sting his IS could have thrown him into anaphylactic shock and killed him. Nonetheless, he still removed wasp nests as a favor to his neighbors, risking his life to save their children from the occasional sting.

Anaphylactic shock is like the extreme form of a hay fever or asthma attack. A relatively harmless pathogen such as pollen triggers massive secretions of histamine in the respiratory tract. In tandem with the effects of aroused nervous and endocrine systems, this inflames the blood vessels, increases the mucus flow and fluid in the lungs, lowers blood pressure and, worst of all, constricts the bronchial passages. In severe cases, the sufferer gasps for air and literally can't breathe.

Either this or the consequences of a dropping pulse rate can lead to death within minutes.

Pollen is just not that dangerous. This response is the result of an immune system gone berserk. It is like burning your house down to get rid of a mouse.

When the Immune System Is Out of Balance

Ideally, the IS would only target pathogens and the cells they inhabit. In fact, it often causes a lot of collateral damage. Inflammation, for example, is an important way the body contains an infection until it is cleaned up, like fencing off the battlefield. But sustained inflammation will also damage healthy cells in the vicinity.

Inflammation is kept in check by the anti-inflammatory corticoids. If they overreact, they suppress the valuable immune function that inflammation performs. This is why they, and the synthetic cortisone people use to control inflammation, are called immunosuppressants. By taking cortisone, you may control a local inflammation, but at the expense of undermining the IS as a whole.

Like officious border guards, the killer T-cells will kill any of our own cells that harbor a virus, whether that virus is harmful or not. The Hepatitis B virus, for example, is relatively benign and does little harm to the liver cells it inhabits. However this scorched earth policy of the IS can systematically destroy the liver itself.

A shaky IS is also dangerous if it fails to adequately distinguish friend and foe. In rheumatoid arthritis, for example, it starts to destroy our own tissues as if they were foreign pathogens.

To recap, the IS is a complex system that is particularly vulnerable to imbalances. It may produce too much or too little inflammation via the adrenal glands. It may destroy cells harboring a virus when it doesn't need to, and target perfectly healthy cells. Its skirmishes frequently cause collateral damage to innocent bystanders.

Most important of all, it gets exhausted and underperforms. Since a weak IS makes us more susceptible to everything, we could argue a case for it as the fundamental cause of disease and ill-health.

Emotions Affect the Immune System

We can't affect our immune systems directly in the same way we can release muscle tension. We can't say, "I think I'll sit down and make a few more million white blood cells," for example. However, we can affect it indirectly.

The IS is particularly responsive to our emotional state. It is well-known that depression and grief will depress the IS and make a person more susceptible to cancer, heart disease, arthritis, respiratory and digestive problems, among others. A good physician, caring for someone recently widowed, knows the patient is entering a high-risk zone for their health.

Conversely, a person who gets excellent emotional support after a bereavement will often show improvement in his or her chronic ailments. The pain of watching someone die often makes the watcher sick, and the death relieves that pressure. This can lead to an actual improvement in health, if the emotional issues are managed well.

Often in adults, asthma first occurs after a traumatic shock. We don't know why a car accident can make a person asthmatic for the rest of their life, but it can. Asthmatics often notice clear connections between their emotional states and their health. When they are upset, their symptoms get worse immediately.

The effects of chronic stress have a visible effect on the IS. The heart will become enlarged, which is a clear sign of disease. The thymus gland, where killer T-cells come to maturity, will shrink. The lymph glands and passages, where most of the biggest battles against disease take place, will also wither.

Whenever we are tense or anxious, the endocrine and nervous systems stir up the body. Many of the hormonal and other responses act as immunosuppressants, and otherwise throw the IS out of kilter. In brief, you can say that if you feel hysterical, your IS will be as well. When we are tense or mentally active the IS is under-resourced.

Helping the Immune System Do Its Work

The IS works best if the body is in homeostasis, which we experience as a state of relaxation. When we are sick, we have a strong instinct to rest and take it easy because this is the environment that supports healing. As a rule of thumb, you can say that when you relax, the body is in self-healing mode.

The IS, like the digestive system, only works well when you are relaxed or asleep. If you are tense most of the day, your IS will be under pressure most of the day. The exercises in this book that encourage you to be relaxed while you go about your ordinary daily activities are thus increasing the amount of time your IS is working well.

You can just ask yourself, "Am I relaxed right now?" or to frame it another way, "Can I do what I am doing in a more relaxed fashion?" With a little practice, you will soon recognize when you are unnecessarily tense or mentally active and shift your body towards homeostasis.

You could also practice "spot-meditations," to defuse tension on the spot. These slow the mind down, bring you into the present and usually enhance your sensory awareness. They can be done while walking, standing or doing simple tasks. They can be very brief, since even a minute's meditation can disarm the chronic thoughts, and you can be quite imaginative and spontaneous with them.

❋

Four Active Meditations

BEING CONSCIOUS OF THE BREATH

Choose some daily activity that has a clear start and finish: showering, dressing, walking to the store or taking out the garbage, for example. Do what you have to do, but be aware of your breathing throughout.

You could count the breaths if you wish, or make the breathing smoother and more regular.

SOUND AND TOUCH

While doing some activity such as brushing your teeth, preparing food or hanging out the washing, focus on the sounds or tactile sensations that arise and savor them. If necessary, say the word "sound" or "touch" each time you breathe out, to remind yourself of your focus.

DOING WHAT YOU ARE DOING

Take some simple activity you usually do automatically: ironing, washing the dishes, feeding the dog, organizing the room. Resolve to be as present as you can, noticing textures, smells, sounds and body sensations consciously. If you wander into irrelevant thinking, focus a little more intently on the next sensation.

SLOWING DOWN

Choose any activity (such as the ones mentioned above), and try to do it just 2% slower (you will still have time to do everything!). By watching how you open a cupboard door, for example, your movements will become a little smoother and more harmonious.

❈

FOURTEEN

Infertility and Sexuality

❈

Meditation helps people enjoy sex more and helps women become pregnant. The reason for the former is fairly obvious. Meditation is a sensual activity. It takes us out of our heads and into our bodies and the sense world around us. It is not surprising that this makes sex more enjoyable.

While most sexually active Westerners now use methods to avoid pregnancy, or delay it until a convenient time, it can be surprisingly difficult to make babies when you want to! About 20% of couples are infertile, and many more struggle for years before succeeding.

Meditation encourages pregnancy by counteracting the destabilizing effect of our all-too-modern lives and restoring homeostasis. A woman is much more likely to become pregnant if the subtle hormonal processes of the reproductive system are working smoothly.

Whether pregnancy occurs or not has always depended on many variables. It is not enough just to bring a man into the equation. Even with regular sex, hardly any woman has the thirty or so children she is theoretically capable of. A woman's body has all kinds of ways of avoiding pregnancy or delaying until a time it deems more appropriate. For some women, unfortunately, the switch seems stuck at the "Off. Not Now" position.

There is no doubt a woman's perception of stress, and actual external stressors, play a major role. Stress affects the reproductive system almost as clearly as it does the cardiovascular system, even if the results are not as immediately obvious. Women undergoing artificial fertilization techniques are commonly encouraged to undertake a stress reduction program as part of the treatment.[1]

As Robin Baker says in his entertaining book *Sperm Wars*, "Stress is a powerful contraceptive." A stressed woman is unconsciously evaluating the external conditions as threatening, and her body responds appropriately. "The more a woman is stressed the less likely she is to ovulate. She is also less likely to help sperm reach the egg or to allow a fertilized egg to implant in her womb. Finally, she is more likely to miscarry, particularly in the first three months of pregnancy."[2]

Sometimes the reduction of stress alone has unexpected results. Last year a student phoned to explain why she couldn't complete her meditation course. She was now pregnant and her morning sickness went all the way through to the evening. "It's your fault," she complained. "I must have relaxed too much!"

By learning to meditate, several of my students have become pregnant, as they wished, and given birth to healthy children. There are several children on this planet who might not be here if their mothers hadn't come to my classes. I find this a little unsettling.

How Stress Hormones Stop Pregnancy

Pregnancy is not something to undertake lightly. It takes a colossal amount of energy—50,000 calories by one estimate (probably an underestimate!). Becoming pregnant at the wrong time can easily be fatal for the infant and the mother as well. As a result, nature in all its wisdom has given the female body many ways of preventing conception, and of aborting the process after it has started.

While the major hormonal players are well known, the outcome in any particular case is unpredictable. Among other things, it depends on external stressors, the woman's conscious perception of stress, and her body's perception (which may be quite different). Having said this, women still conceive in concentration camps and others are barren while living happily in a paradise.

As women know, their monthly cycle is mediated by a sequence of hormones. Via a hormone that I will mercifully abbreviate to LHRH, the hypothalamus triggers the pituitary to release Follicle Stimulating Hormone (FSH), which brings the ovum to maturity in the ovary. By the same pathway, Luteinizing Hormone (LH) releases the ovum into the fallopian tube at the right time—the prerequisite for a fertile cycle. After this mini-explosion in the midst of the cycle, the ovaries produce less estrogen and more progesterone, preparing the uterine walls to receive a fertilized egg.[3]

Stress can easily throw out the complex timing involved. If there are too many disturbances, the result is likely to be an anovulatory cycle in which the woman has a period, but without an egg being released. A ripening ovum will easily go on hold and remain in the ovary until next time.

We know that many of the stress hormones inhibit the reproductive process. Endorphins (a side effect of stress) inhibit LHRH release, and prolactin, a stress hormone from the pituitary, inhibits uptake of LHRH.

Prolactin has a clear contraceptive effect by suppressing estrogen and progesterone. As its name suggests, it is stimulated by breast feeding. "Demand-feeding," if allowed to occur dozens of times a day as naturally happens in pre-industrial societies, is an excellent form of birth control. Stress also maintains high levels of prolactin in the body.[4]

Many women starve themselves in the name of fashion or sport. The skin-and-bones model and the muscular sportswoman are both liable to retarded sexual development, anovulatory cycles and sometimes a complete halt to menstruation. Both the languid model and the hyper-energetic sportswoman are putting their bodies under enormous stress. They become infertile because their bodies know that pregnancy would be dangerous for their health in these circumstances.

From their adrenals, women secrete small amounts of male hormones that suppress reproduction if their levels get too high. For a normal woman, these hormones are disarmed and converted to estrogen via enzymes in their fat cells. In a state of fashion- or sport-induced starvation, however, the fat cells are depleted and male hormone levels rise. You don't want to become pregnant if you are caught in a famine.[5]

Fertile bodies need ample reserves to support another being inside them. The average man, with his appetite for curves, instinctively knows this. Curvaceous women are more likely to be fertile. You may be fashionably slender, but the scientific evidence suggests that putting on a few extra pounds could help you get pregnant.

Sunk in Mid-stream

Once a fertilized egg is floating down the fallopian tubes towards the uterus, it is still not plain sailing by any means. We may sentimentally feel that all life is precious, but nature doesn't seem to agree. Many eggs never implant and many abort in the first month or two. A woman may have been temporarily pregnant many times without realizing. Perhaps less than one in a hundred fertilized eggs make it to birth, though no one really knows the number.

In other words, a woman's body can often halt the process after it has started. Some mammals, such as rabbits, will spontaneously abort to control the timing of their pregnancies and birth. Others commonly abort in cases of shock or stress. A stock figure in literature is the young woman who tragically miscarries because of unbearable emotional strain.

While prolactin is implicated here, a couple of old familiar villains return to the scene—adrenaline and noradrenaline. As we know, the stress response diverts blood flow away from unessential functions such as digestion. Unfortunately, this also means the fetus can suffer a sudden loss of blood flow and oxygen. In such cases, the blood pressure drops and heart rate slows down.

If this occurs just occasionally, there is unlikely to be any bad effect at all, but the process is dangerous. The loss of pressure and oxygen is what causes a heart to stop beating when we hemorrhage, for example. The heart suffocates from lack of oxygen. It makes cruel sense that repeated instances of this may kill the fetus. The body is getting the message: "It's getting very dangerous out there—too dangerous to be pregnant."

Preparing the Body for Pregnancy

Anything that helps you relax and manage your stress better will help you get pregnant. A sympathetic doctor or family, a support group or stress-management strategy, cutting down your workload, intelligent use of leisure time and more of it, and good sex will all help. And meditation is an obvious skill for enhancing all of these.

Self-awareness and listening to your body will help a lot. One of my students suffered repeated miscarriages until she realized she could do something about it. She simplified her life, learned to meditate and how to be relaxed during the day, and treated herself kindly. She came to class walking on eggshells, knowing she would miscarry again if she got too anxious. It was a huge triumph for her to get pregnant and carry the baby through to its birth.

She knew she had to create a healthy internal environment for pregnancy. The baby's first nursery is its mother's womb, and this has to feel like a safe and nourishing place. No matter how much a woman wants a child, if she is chronically anxious, her body is saying "Danger! Watch out! Be on your guard." It may also be saying "This is no time to make babies!" She had to convince her own body that it was safe to be pregnant, and to persuade the embryo to stay.

Many women are at war with their own bodies. I particularly notice women who lock up in the diaphragm. They have a permanent knot of dread (or a rock, or a lead ball, as some have described it) in their solar plexus. They may be able to relax the rest of their bodies, but they still hold on here.

A muscular lock usually means, "I can't handle this. I don't want to know about it. I'm going to ignore it." At least some of this tension relates to what happens below the rib cage, particularly digestion and sexuality.

If this happens, it means there is very little juice or positive emotionality going towards the sexual organs. The blood supply literally diminishes as the organs and adjacent muscles tighten up under the stress response. Many women can't consider this part of their bodies without profound anxiety. And they are trying to grow a baby in there?

The trauma is often genuine. Our sexual history often carries damage and pain. The meditation teacher Steven Levine taught a meditation with a title like "Washing the Womb with Light." One imagined light or loving energy flowing into all the dark corners, cleansing the traumas and healing the memories embedded in the flesh. Until these emotions are released, it can be difficult to enjoy sex.

Though a woman can obviously get pregnant while not enjoying intercourse at all, it seems probable that the pleasure can help. During sex, the blood flow increases and the whole region is massaged by rhythmic movement. We know that muscles, and presumably organs as well, can't be put on the shelf until needed. They need to be used regularly and enjoyed to be healthy.

Once a woman is pregnant, she still needs to be careful. Her stress hormones go right through the placenta, whether she wants them to or not. The fetus probably doesn't like this endocrine bath any more than we do. Stress inhibits the production of growth hormone in an adult body and probably affects a fetus similarly. Too much adrenaline doesn't feel good either.

Embryos and fetuses are what the Japanese call "water-babies." Water, as we know from physics, is the ultimate receptor. It will pick up the tiniest signals and influences from its environment. We know that unborn children, being mostly water, are hypersensitive to environmental toxins. They are likewise bound to be affected by the biochemistry of their mothers.

Preparing for Birth

Many women take up meditation when they become pregnant. I have had many unborn children in my classes (for some reason, they often become quite active when their mothers relax!).

Pregnancy causes huge biochemical changes and a diversion of energy in the body. A woman who listens to her body learns to monitor those changes and pace herself appropriately. After the birth, she is less likely to be at the mercy of the mood swings that new mothers are famous for.

In childbirth, meditation can help in two ways. A woman can partially detach from the pain while still being fully aware of it. She can be both the spectator and the heroine of the drama.

She can also physically relax into the process. When the contractions begin, the upper part of the womb is tightening. Paradoxically, at the same time the lower part needs to relax, so the cervix can open. If she is calm and aware, and trusts her body (because as a meditator she knows it well) she will be able to contract at the top and release at the bottom.

On the other hand, if she is caught in fear and pain, she will tend to tighten everywhere, including the cervix (this tends to occur in premenstrual cramps as well). Rather than relaxing, the cervix will hold on until it is painfully forced open by the pressure of the infant's head.

From my observations, if women are at ease with themselves during pregnancy and birth, the infants tend to be at peace with themselves too. After birth, they face the outer world with confidence. It may be just coincidence, but they tend to be good sleepers, healthy, lively and curious—just like babies should be.

Male Sexual Dysfunction

Men are much simpler creatures as far as reproduction is concerned, though some similar processes apply. The endorphins released through stress will inhibit our Follicle Stimulating Hormones and Luteinising Hormones. Despite their feminine names, FSH and LH encourage testosterone and sperm production. If we are under stress, or stressing the body as elite athletes do, our fertility is definitely impaired.

We can get lost in technicalities while talking of female reproduction. However, most male sexual problems are emotional in nature, which brings us back to the key point. For both men and women, it is our emotions that originally stimulate the stress response. Therefore, how can we relax and enjoy life, and more specifically, how can we enjoy sex?

Huge numbers of men are sexually dysfunctional, or the act is so fraught with anxiety that they no longer attempt it. While we are often accused of just wanting to get our rocks off, we do know the difference between good sex and bad sex.

Some men ejaculate too soon for their own enjoyment, let alone that of their partner. Since the moment of ejaculation is triggered by the sympathetic nervous system, this suggests that stress is implicated. Other men have orgasms, but their erections are too soft or short-lived for real pleasure. Some men can't get erect at all, or suffer periodic impotence.

It is almost impossible for a man to have an erection unless he relaxes. An anxious thought can wilt an erection within seconds. But how can you relax when you are thinking, "Am I going to be able to make it or not? And will she enjoy it?"

Sex therapists know the best cure for performance anxiety is to relax and take it easy. The veins in the penis have to relax to allow the blood to flow in and stiffen the tissues. If you just cuddle and kiss and don't care what happens, it often happens. As you relax, the blood flows to the extremities and the genitals come alive. This is also why men have erections when they sleep.

When we meditate and relax, there is more blood flow to the periphery of the body. Blood drains from the big muscles that control movement and flows out to the skin and to the digestive system. People usually notice this as a gentle tingling or warmth on the skin.

For both sexes, adrenaline reduces the blood supply to the sexual organs, and relaxation increases it. Just as the bowels loosen somewhat when you meditate, so there can be a pleasant warmth in the genitals. They often feel alive and comfortable, even if there is no strong sexual component. Perhaps because meditation is supposed to be a "spiritual" activity, books rarely mention this sensual flavor.

Meditation shifts you out of your head into your body. While doing nothing at all—just sitting on a chair or cushion—your body sinks into a more physical, sensual and occasionally a sexual zone. It is not so much lustful, but more like that feeling of completeness you get *after* good sex. Nonetheless, it is subtle and meditators may not realize why they feel so good. If you do meditate, you may like to ask yourself, "Do I feel more like making love before or after I meditate?" The effect will probably be obvious to you.

This meditative feeling is the perfect precursor to leisurely lovemaking. I did several long retreats when I was young, and the unexpected improvement in my sex life was a huge bonus. Meditation seems to make our natural instinct for pleasure more alive and intelligent. It is not surprising that the Indian teacher Osho developed sexual meditations (involving very playful foreplay) to open the heart and body simultaneously.

Relaxation and Enjoyment

Relaxation speaks to the body about safety, comfort and pleasure. To enjoy sex or pregnancy the body has to relax, and the more the better. The rhythms of intimacy and lovemaking should be slow and leisurely. Doctors used to recommend that if couples wanted to get pregnant, they should take a long holiday, away from the jagged edges of city life. A less expensive option is to meditate.

If a man wants a child, he can't just tell his wife he loves her. His words may not trickle down to her womb. He needs to be affectionate enough to convince her body, and not just her mind, that it is loved. It also helps if he is comfortable with the physicality of his own body.

Healthy sexual pleasure also sends positive emotional signals completely through the bodies of both partners. The boundaries between self and other blur. You enjoy your own body as much as your partner's. You wash yourself in good feeling that is both physical and emotional. For a while at least, you love yourself in the direct non-verbal way that you felt your mother's love as an infant. This is the emotional tone of a fertile couple.

Our sexual organs are designed for both conception and pleasure. It doesn't make sense to try to divorce these two functions. It seems likely that pleasure promotes conception by energizing the sexual organs, by making the woman feel good about herself, and by making her feel loved by the man whose support she will probably need. As I discuss in Chapter 16, pleasure is an excellent way to activate the relaxation response.

Sexual Meditations

There are many ways to meditate for sexual function and pregnancy. The basic aim is to relax and enhance a sense of pleasure in the body. Most meditations should produce this as a secondary effect at least. For the above purposes, however, it should become a primary focus.

An obvious way to do this is sexual fantasy. This has all the hallmarks of a good meditation object. It focuses the mind well and takes you from thinking into sensing. Like any body-based meditation, you can also read the signs of success easily. Just make sure you go about it in a relaxed fashion.

Many people will find they relax and enjoy sex more as a fantasy than with another person. Even if you have a good sex life, you usually can't make love every time you feel sexy. Fantasy in solitude allows the positive effects of sexual feeling to ripple through your life without always needing resolution.

A woman trying to become pregnant may do well to meditate on her womb, using meditations that suit her personality. A tactile type may imagine stroking or caressing or feeling good energy flowing through her reproductive organs. A verbal type may use an affirmation or even talk to her womb while doing so. If she is pregnant, she could also talk to her baby. After all, her body is already communicating with it.

A visually oriented person may "see" a warm pink color around the organs. Alternatively, she could imagine the color and texture of healthy ovaries, fallopian tubes and uterus, in as much detail as possible. A few minutes researching the anatomy books is a useful prompt, and photos can help too.

It is not particularly useful to tell or order the body to get pregnant. The body and mind are far too sophisticated to respond to such a crude approach. The essence of any of these meditations is to relax deeply, enjoy the good feeling and let the mind settle. If you want to get pregnant, this is bound to help.

✳

FIFTEEN

Worry, Panic and Compulsions

✳

Worrying is useful. We need a certain vigilance to look after ourselves in an ever-changing world. This is the natural anxiety that goes with being alive.

However, between a quarter to a half of the population worries too much, and their anxiety becomes toxic. Worry is just an intellectual form of fear, and fear can make us completely irrational. We fret about little things that don't matter or about big things we can't control. We become overly shy and cautious, terrified of making mistakes. We become perfectionists, or feel incapable of doing anything right.

We lose perspective and respond to little things just as much as to big things. We imagine the worst scenarios and see slights, disasters and embarrassment everywhere. We even suffer "free-floating" anxiety. Our habitual body arousal convinces us that something is wrong, so we go looking for something to worry about. But as one man said, "I am an old man and I've had lots of worries—most of which never happened."

This toxic anxiety directly impacts the body. A habitual worrier is likely to have elevated levels of stress hormones for decades. Keeping the body on red alert is exhausting, and we want to just collapse at times. The combination of exhaustion and worry often leads to depression. You have a feeling that you can't cope or go on like this (which is quite true).

Because worriers are in a state of constant low-level fear, they are rarely happy. Their happiness, such as it is, comes from feeling safe and in control, which is always an uncertain proposition. I find many worriers come to learn meditation just because they feel miserable and haven't really enjoyed themselves for years.

Because worry is such a strain on the body, it tends to get worse over the years (before fading in old age). Childhood worrying gradually grows into habitual anxiety which can erupt as panic attacks, obsessive-compulsive disorders or phobias. Worriers typically suffer for decades before they fully realize how destructive their behavior is.

Meditation can help throughout the entire spectrum of mild worry to life-degrading neuroses. Because worriers usually start so young, they are unlikely to completely stop worrying. "Once a worrier, always a worrier."

However, they can dissolve their toxic anxiety and become healthy worriers. They can worry about the right things to the right degree and let go of responsibility for what is beyond their control. Thus they become rational worriers, and turn their natural tendency into a useful skill.

Meditation helps in several ways. Worriers think too much. Meditation shifts them from thinking to sensing. Worry elevates nervous system arousal and stress hormone levels. Relaxing reduces these. Worry ties itself up in knots. Meditation gives you clarity and perspective, so you look at a problem without too much fear confusing the issue.

When Worry Is Bad for Our Health

Our bodies need to rest periodically to function well and repair the damage of a busy day. The body of a chronically anxious person, however, may never return to homeostasis, or even be in allostatic balance. If you are suffering from troublesome symptoms with causes that cannot be found on the usual tests, it is possible that chronic anxiety may be behind it. Just as unresolved emotion is often the hidden source of pain, so anxiety can express itself in an array of ailments.

No one likes to be told, "You're not sick. You're just too anxious." It implies that you can't cope with life, and many worriers see themselves as very good copers—perfectionists, even.

Anxiety alone may not cause an illness, but it often exacerbates an existing condition. If a doctor can't find any physiological reasons behind your heart arrhythmia or intestinal upset or chronic pain, she may well feel that your anxiety is the culprit. Depending on your personality, it can impinge on virtually any part of the body.

In *Healing the Anxiety Diseases,* Dr. Leaman maps out the physiological effects of severe anxiety. In the muscles it can emerge as fatigue, generalized pain, headaches and muscle spasm. It can cause constricted breathing and hyperventilation. It may be implicated in most intestinal disorders—indigestion, gas, pain, diarrhea and constipation, lack of appetite and heartburn. It can cause heart palpitations and chest pain. And so on.[1]

Panic and Anxiety Attacks

If your anxiety level has been high for months, it can erupt as a panic attack, often out of the blue. Panic attacks can even occur in a completely stress-free situation like a quiet street, or sitting alone in your living room.

Your body is paralyzed. You flush with heat and sweat. You may feel lightheaded, nauseous and suffocated. The breath is trapped in the first two stages of arousal, as described in Chapter 8. Your breathing is frozen or hyperventilating (short rapid in-breaths) or both.

When it first happens, you may think you are about to die or have a heart attack. The episode may only last a few seconds before subsiding, but the blow to your self-esteem and the shock of becoming so dysfunctional can be devastating. The attack itself was bad enough, but now you have the added fear of it happening again.

You now play out the scenarios. What happens if you freeze in a meeting or a supermarket? What happens if you flush, can't breathe or talk, and feel like you're about to vomit or collapse on the spot? You panic about your tendency to panic.

Fortunately, worriers are also thinkers, and eventually they figure out what to do. They learn the emergency strategies, while also finding ways to reduce their overall anxiety levels.

While panic attacks are terrifying, the crisis tends to pass quickly, usually within seconds. Once victims realize this, they know they only have to wait and do as little as possible. Just like a good meditator, they stop trying to solve the problem, and instead switch into "watching mode." They watch the panic without panicking.

There are many simple techniques to get through the first few seconds: count to ten, look at the pattern on the carpet, listen to the sounds around you, say a phrase to yourself. The attack itself is screaming, "Emergency! Do something!" By doing something trivial instead, you learn not to respond to that call. If you just wait, the attack passes.

There is one thing you can usefully do. The frozen or hyperventilating breath of panic results in too much in-breathing. If possible, when you panic you should gently connect with the breath.

Try to breathe a little more regularly and slowly, with special emphasis on the out-breath. When you are starting to sigh (indicating that you are enacting the relaxation response), you know you have broken the panic. To stabilize yourself, you finish with gentle regular breathing, with longer out-breaths than in-breaths.

Once people know they can ride out a panic attack, they don't need to be so terrified of it. Now they can look at the primary cause—their chronically high levels of anxiety. If they can just reduce those by 10 to 20%, they may still be tense, but not tense enough to trigger panic attacks.

Learning to relax can seem alien to chronically anxious people. But if their tension is severe enough to cause panic attacks, they are usually highly motivated and determined. In my experience they do surprisingly well in meditation.

Obsessive-Compulsive Disorders

Some people develop rituals to help ward off stress. The childish logic goes, "If I can do this activity several times a day, I will be safe." They can defuse their rising anxiety if they can wash their hands or reorganize the cupboards or check the house security once again.

Habits and rituals have the effect of making life feel predictable and safe, and most of us use them unconsciously. However, obsessive-compulsive behavior takes these habits to a dysfunctional extreme. It is hard to lead a normal life if you have to clean the kitchen surfaces ten times a day to allay your anxiety.

When anxiety is high, the person's ritual behavior increases. It typically flares up in times of external stress. If she is less anxious and life is running smoothly, it decreases.

If a sufferer learns to be more relaxed during the day, the latent anxiety that triggers the behavior decreases. Since meditation also relieves that anxiety, it serves exactly the same function as the compulsive behavior and can eventually replace it.

I am always optimistic when someone comes to learn meditation to help with an obsessive-compulsive disorder. Such persons usually do very well. Being creatures of habit and ritual, they become obsessive about being relaxed. More than any other group of students I know, when they see the benefits, they do the practice and get the results.

Phobias

Some worriers get fixated on just one thing. All their anxiety is directed at dirt, or moths, or open spaces, or bacteria, or cats. They get all the symptoms of a panic attack if faced with one of these. Such people can use meditation to combat the phobia through desensitizing exercises.

For example, a person may be afraid of birds. So he sits in his car and meditates while also watching the seagulls. Safely inside his car, he learns to defuse his anxiety response. Then, carefully, keeping the car door open for a quick retreat, he sits outside on the bench and continues to keep his body and mind relaxed.

He is gradually reprogramming his mind. He now knows it is possible to see birds and still remain relaxed. While he may not be completely fearless next time he is close to birds, he at least knows he has options that seemed impossible before. And this may be all he needs.

Addictive Behavior

Addicts are also compulsive types, trying to escape their latent anxiety. But unlike sufferers of panic attacks and phobias, they fixate not on the worry but on the escape from it.

When we feel really bad, we hunger for something that will make us feel good. It could be food, alcohol, sex, gambling, work, cigarettes, helping others, shopping, housecleaning, playing golf or watching TV.

These things actually work. They do make us feel good—temporarily. Unfortunately, the twentieth chocolate tastes nowhere near as good as the first. But an addict can't resist the twenty-first.

The writer William Burroughs claimed that we are all addicted, if only to ideas and beliefs. He said the best addictions, from a dealer's point of view, are ones we are unconscious of. Ideally, we assume that our daily intake of alcohol, tobacco and the mind drugs of the mass media are perfectly natural.

Almost all of us use mind-altering substances on a daily basis. A survey of French people showed that about half drank alcohol each day, and about half smoked. Two-thirds drank coffee or tea. One-third used prescription drugs to sleep or wake up or feel good. Less than 2% of the population used nothing at all. They were generally regarded as weirdos. This profile is probably true of most Western nations.

Given that most of us have at least a tendency towards addiction and habitual behavior, the secret is to be moderate about it. This can completely change the quality of an addiction. Many heroin addicts and alcoholics, for example, are able to lead fairly normal lives.

Addictions usually include elements of denial and illusory thinking. If, however, you open your eyes and see exactly what is happening, it is harder to be so enthusiastic and single-minded about your drug of choice. It is not so easy to drink to excess the way you used to.

A meditator, whether he likes it or not, comes to know himself better in time. If you sit with yourself, year after year, you come to see your body, your emotions and your thoughts with great depth. You also see "karma," or the consequences of your actions.

The Indian teacher Osho gave a smoking meditation that was based on the Buddhist maxim, "when eating, just eat." In this case he said, smoke a cigarette giving 100% attention to all the sensations.

It starts before you even light up. You notice the longing in the mind. Then the anticipation, the sounds, the smell, the feeling of the smoke in the lungs, the consequent change in consciousness and, when the cigarette is over, the feeling afterwards. If you are honest with yourself, you find that many of those sensations and feelings are not pleasant.

This kind of clear-seeing attention may help break an addiction, which usually depends on a blind, automatic, slightly hypnotic state of mind. You may still enjoy smoking, but you are unlikely to puff through sixty a day.

Counterindications

Useful as meditation is for many kinds of mental distress, it still has its limits. It is rarely helpful for those people (perhaps 2–5% of the population) who suffer severe mental disturbances. For most people, meditation is either helpful or harmless. For the mentally ill, however, it can be counterproductive.

Usually such people don't have the discipline to meditate anyway, so the question doesn't arise. If they do, however, it can exacerbate their behavior. People with paranoid tendencies can become more paranoid, and the clinically depressed even more so.

Borderline schizophrenics, who commonly have a tendency to solitude and withdrawal, often find their way into meditation groups. Because meditation tends to loosen one's sense of self and expand the mind, schizophrenics can seriously lose the plot. The best advice any meditation teacher can give a schizophrenic is, "Don't meditate!"

Meditation can work well for people with a borderline mental disorder, but professional care is still needed. I often work in conjunction with psychiatrists. They provide the cognitive and chemical supports; I teach the physical skill and detached awareness.

Summary

For all the people I cover in this chapter, from worriers to sufferers of panic attacks, from obsessive-compulsive victims to addicts, it helps to be able to relax consciously. Those of my students who have used meditation to give up smoking or alcohol usually say things like "I wanted some other way to relieve anxiety and feel good."

However, relaxing alone is not enough. The underlying causes of anxiety go very deep, and worriers also want to understand what they are. To put it bluntly, it is quite easy to talk a chronically anxious person through a relaxation exercise and get them to rest. But they don't stay in that state because it doesn't feel like their true identity.

Worriers are thinkers. To feel good they need to have a good mental grasp of who they are and what is going on around them. The greater benefits they get from meditation are a sense of detachment and clarity. Meditation helps them see their problems without the usual fear and anger responses that so befuddle the brain. They no longer confuse the mountains with the molehills.

Some degree of anxiety is a natural response to the uncertain world around us, but it doesn't need to become toxic. Habitual worry, by definition, is unbalanced thinking. It dissolves when your mind is relaxed and clear.

❁

Rotating the Worries

A worrier can usually find plenty to worry about, and each worry tends to suck him in before he moves on to the next one. This little meditation helps neutralize that effect.

While you meditate, you also notice your worries and itemize them. You notice what you are worrying about at any particular moment and you give it a label such as "work" or "death" or "taxes" or "baldness." If you want, you can imagine putting the labeled worry on a shelf.

Instead of dwelling on it, you notice what else you are worrying about. You name that also—"Peter" or "getting fat" or "tachycardia"—and move on to the next worry.

Fairly soon you have six or eight worries lined up on the shelf. Instead of getting drawn into any one, let your mind move lightly from one to the other. Now play with them. Go through them from left to right, or right to left. You may notice that they all have different emotional charges. This sense of distance and choice is all you need to diffuse their power.

✳

SIXTEEN

Smart Sensuality

✳

When we relax, we shift into healing mode. Some events, however, can initiate that shift very rapidly. They are moments of delight, when the whole body goes "Aaahhh." Here are some examples.

You rush out of the house, glad to escape the squabbling kids and irritable wife at the breakfast table. As you stand still to open the car door, you feel the breeze caress your cheek. It seems like the earth is gently breathing over you. And you realize the trees above are alive with birds.

You lie in pain on a hospital bed, coming to terms with what your operation has done to you. Through the inner turmoil you hear an old song on the radio. It plucks you from the room and takes you back forty years, flooding you with memories.

You feel tired and harried, so you mechanically make a cup of tea. You sit down, lift it to your lips and—miracle of miracles—you actually taste it! It's just delicious. You wonder why you didn't do it earlier.

You are grieving a death in the family. Amid the other mail, you find a beautiful card from a friend. It stops time for a moment and tears come to your eyes, even though you can't say why.

You have a massage and feel your body responding like a cat being stroked. You know the masseuse is just doing her job for the money, and probably thinking about the weekend, but it doesn't seem to matter. Her touch seems to carry faint memories of all the good touching you've ever known.

You struggle resentfully through your aerobics or yoga class, not wanting to be there. But as you chat with classmates at the end, you realize you are all smiling and your body feels great.

What Makes a Moment of Grace?

Such moments are like being touched by an angel. Though brief, their after-effects can last all day. For some people they are very rare. For others, they are common ingredients of any day. We can't turn them on at will, but we can prepare the conditions for them to happen.

Most feel good for both the heart and the body. They come via sensation and evoke emotion. Both aspects are valuable, but in this chapter I want to emphasize the importance of the sensual component.

Sensing comes first, and is very direct in its effect. Emotion, on the other hand, is often a kind of secondary contemplation of actual sensations. You could even say that emotion is more of a pleasing memory than the real thing. Nonetheless, the memories can be richer than the real thing.

The body is a more sensual animal than the mind. If you want to shift its chemistry into healing mode, you give it lovely things to smell, taste, see, hear and feel. If the body is feeling pleasure, the emotional tone will probably be healthy as well.

The body is more childlike than the mind. This has huge advantages in terms of healing. Little children are more sensual than adults, and their emotions are less divorced from their bodies. If you give an upset child a cuddle, she often responds well. She feels loved, even though you at that moment may also be feeling annoyed with her.

If a child, or our own body, is in a state of pleasure, it rather blindly projects its positive feeling into the environment. As far as the body is concerned, it doesn't matter if Mommy really loves you, or if the friend who sent the card did it out of affection or duty. It is much easier to trick the body into healing mode than to con the mind.

For a little child, love and enjoyment are very physical matters. They come through being repeatedly touched and fed and talked to and stimulated and cared for. Generally, the more physical the parenting is, the more the child will instinctively feel loved.

If a child has a rich sensual interaction with the world, she will tend to see it as a safe and interesting place rather than a hostile one. Conversely, a parent who may be very fond of her child but doesn't express it physically may raise a child who always feels unsafe and fearful. In other words, one child is primed to feel relaxed and the other is primed to feel tense.

Relaxing through the Senses

If as adults we want to evoke that body-feeling of safety and enjoyment, we can largely do it through the senses. Unfortunately, we try to do it more through our thoughts, and this mutes the effect. For example, we may get pleasure out of gardening not because it is enjoyable in itself but because we like the idea of a tidy garden.

The body, however, doesn't give a damn about that. If it feels good after gardening it is more because of the sensual contact. It feels good to touch the rough bark of tree prunings, or the clamminess of moist earth, or to see the tiny flower of some weed that has managed to survive despite our best efforts to eradicate it.

The body, like a small child, has atavistic appetites. It relishes the smell of manure, the stickiness of sweat, the crunch of dead leaves in the hand. Even sunburn or a scratch on the skin can feel delicious as well as painful.

We often try to enjoy things more in our heads than in our bodies. We make love more interested in how it affects the on-going mind games of the relationship than in the physicality of the moment. This is a sophisticated adult approach to sex but it may not satisfy the body.

As far as the body is concerned, sex is about warmth and smells, about the squeeze and slither of flesh and skin, about stickiness and saliva. If we can let the body enjoy all of this with the natural self-centeredness of a little child, it will feel nourished, even if the relationship as a whole is a mess. When Chinese doctors used to prescribe sex as a medicine for certain ailments, complete with times and doses, they knew what they were doing.

Many people of a spiritual bent suffer from "sensation-hunger." They alienate themselves, deliberately or unconsciously, from the natural pleasure of the body. But even a nun, untouched since childhood, knows what it is like to be held in a total embrace of unconditional love. That was her experience while in her mother's womb, and her mother couldn't even help it!

Just as our musculature needs to move for good health, so our senses need to be adequately activated. A diet of words and "important matters" is thin gruel, and the body gets sick on it.

Pleasure Works like Meditation

Meditators often aim for a state of "samadhi," which means "oneness" or "absorption." This is when the meditation object fills consciousness so completely that everything else temporarily vanishes. The feeling is generally one of profound peace, pleasure and space. While pure samadhi rarely lasts more than a few seconds, it is lovely just to be in its vicinity.

At these moments you are alert, but your habitual thoughts and sense of self are eclipsed. You actually "stand outside" yourself, which is the literal meaning of the word "ecstasy." These transpersonal moments are delightful because our sense of self, and the worries that invariably circulate around it, has vanished. The actual meditation object doesn't matter.

Moments of pleasure, however, can have much the same effect. At the moment your teeth pierce the skin of the nectarine and the juice spills over your tongue, where are your problems then? This small moment of ecstasy takes you out of yourself and triggers the relaxation response.

Just as the meditator becomes one with the breath, so you become one with the nectarine. The mind flows into an unconditional embrace in which everything is momentarily perfect. Both meditation and pleasure induce a sense of oneness.

Anxiety, in contrast, is characterized by separation and duality. Anger is trying to get rid of something. Fear is a retreat from something. Desire is wanting something you haven't got. All of these painful emotions can be dissolved in a moment of pleasure.

Smart Sensuality

When we are anxious, we unconsciously seek out pleasure to counteract this sense of separation. We want to eat or smoke or initiate contact by talking. Very often, however, the pleasure is contaminated by the anxiety we carry. True pleasure comes and goes spontaneously, and is easily strangled if we try to hang on to it.

We can, however, develop a sense of "smart sensuality." Instead of grabbing at pleasure, we give ourselves opportunities and time for it to arise. We also learn to value pleasure. Instead of lightly admiring the flowering creeper as we walk by, we pause and savor it more deeply. We know that this little act nourishes our body and soul and keeps us closer to that relaxed mode in which healing occurs.

When people feel burnt-out by decades of head-dominated careers, they often seek balance by doing earthy, nonverbal things. They take up painting or carpentry or gardening or tai chi or dancing or singing—the kind of things they left behind in their youth.

A retired executive may want to simply do handyman work for months. A friend of mine, on leaving her demanding career, went through the whole gamut of rebalancing activities: going to classes on massage, aromatherapy, herbalism, painting, while also redesigning the garden, joining a choir, indulging her passion for food and attending as many concerts as she possibly could.

Why is it so relaxing to paint, for example? First, you have to focus on what you are doing or the result will be a mess. Second, there is something deeply sensual and immediate about watching ribbons of paint transfer from brush to canvas. This is a little world of its own, rich in color, smell, texture and its own organic rhythms that have nothing to do with the outer world. The mind is focused in the present and sensing, just as in meditation.

Sensuality as Therapy

The unconscious message in a moment of pleasure is, "This is it. Everything is okay. You can relax now." Pleasure is worth cultivating intelligently. You can even regard it as a kind of body/mind medicine. There are many ways you could go about this.

The first is to grasp the moment. When something beautiful catches your senses, consciously enjoy it. You can always give a few extra seconds to the smell of the coffee, to the touch of a chile pepper, to the splash of tap water, to the texture of skin conditioner, to the elegance of a well-cut dress or a lovely face.

I do this consciously as a spontaneous meditation. When something attracts me, I hit the pause button in the mind and give the object total attention—often for just five seconds. I absorb it with my whole body, and often imprint it in memory as well. I hold it in the mind for a few seconds after the occasion has passed, and often recall it later in the day.

These moments are like little drops of nectar. They are small but deeply nourishing, and you can enjoy scores of them each day. After they pass, the mind feels clear and bright, before the habitual thinking gets going again. Without these moments of delight, the day (and the months and years ahead) can seem unremittingly bleak. In the grey-black world of depression there is little color to interrupt the gloom.

Secondly, you can do things that create the opportunity for pleasure. This is where you deliberately set aside time, at least once a day, to do something you enjoy. Some people need the structure of a yoga class or the ritual of a daily walk. Others prefer to improvise.

It is pleasant enough to waffle along, more or less enjoying ourselves. But we get more out of it if we consciously seek those moments of bright sensation. These are the circuit breakers that stop dead the habit of mental chatter.

A moment of deep sensing can follow all the guidelines of a good meditation: you consciously focus and don't let the mind wander. You enhance your awareness of the object, enjoying it in detail. You let your whole body relax into the experience.

In general, a few seconds of high-definition sensing is more valuable than a few minutes of being more or less relaxed. It can induce a huge shift in your quality of mind. Just a few seconds can bring back the freshness of perception we enjoyed as children and remind us how lovely the world can be.

A Connoisseur of Simple Things

Monks and nuns are assumed to lead lives of deprivation: no sex, no entertainment, little food. In fact they may be leading lives of refined sensuality. They have time to feel the morning air on their faces, to watch the wind moving through the trees and to feel the pleasure of their body moving.

Years ago, at the end of a teaching term, I used to have a meal with 60 to 80 meditators at a friend's restaurant. Since it was a smorgasbord, people could eat as much as they liked. My friend said that, for us, he always prepared less food than usual.

Meditators tend to taste their food. They know how their bodies feel and so they don't like to eat too much. The usual customers, on the other hand, would eat a lot. They would go back for a second or third plate because they had been too mentally busy to enjoy the first.

When we drop the inner conversations, we enter a world rich in feeling and sensing. We can re-enter the mindstate of a little child. Smells, tastes, sounds, sights and textures become vivid and satisfying. We talk, but we enjoy the food as well. We drive home from work, but still enjoy the sunset. We know what gives us real pleasure and don't just blindly consume. A meditator can be an epicure of simple things. For these reasons alone, meditators tend to be happier people.

An Expansive and Adaptable Mind

Meditators commonly have a dreadful habit of meditating on just one object for years. This can be boring, to say the least, which is why people don't meditate as much as they feel they should. This single-mindedness goes against the natural tendency of the mind to explore and know.

The holy men and women of the Buddha's day, however, trained to focus on anything at hand. Like them, you could meditate, for example, on the sparkle of light on water; shadow patterns; the wind in the grass; the sound of rain; your heartbeat; the sensations of urination or defecation; the feel of the earth under your feet; a twig or pebble or fleck of dirt; decaying flowers or a decomposing animal; the sound, smell, taste and texture of food as you eat it; sky, space and clouds; the steam from boiling water; the breeze on your skin; fire and smoke; heat and cold; the coming and going of pleasant and unpleasant sensations in the body; sunlight and moonlight; and the primary and secondary colors.

There were formal instructions for all these meditation objects and hundreds more. Even so, it was considered better to do them informally, as the occasion arose. It is not difficult to get high-quality awareness and clarity of mind in a short, spontaneous meditation. All you have to do is use what catches your attention during the day.

※

Visual Object

Let your eyes choose anything in your field of vision. It could be something beautiful (a leaf, a cloud, a person) or something quite ordinary (a stone, or someone's shoe).

Gently examine the detail of it, noticing shape, color, texture and patterns of light, to keep your mind occupied. Keep your eyes soft, and blink as much as you need to. Play with the object in your imagination if you wish. Enjoy any associations that arise. Use the pleasure to keep yourself focused. Have fun in a slow, lazy way.

Don't try to shut out other thoughts and sensations. It helps to keep a background awareness of your body so you don't strain after the object. Check that your breathing is loose and the body is actually relaxing. Let your attention go between your body and the object.

PART THREE

Healing the Mind

❄

SEVENTEEN

An Instinct for Health

❄

For too many of us, health is more of a concept than a feeling. We approach health cerebrally, by reading books about it rather than feeling it in our bodies. When we get sick, we tend to seek information from our doctors rather than listening to what our bodies are telling us. We can intellectually know a lot about health and sickness while barely noticing what either of them feel like.

There are some people who have a deep, visceral instinct for health. They automatically avoid food, activities and thoughts that undermine that feeling. Almost without effort, they avoid what is bad for them and do what feels good. They eat, sleep, work, play and rest with moderation and balance. They generally have trim bodies and a healthy disposition.

Such people often appear disciplined, but this may not be the case. They just have a heightened sense of health, and unhealthy things don't give them any pleasure.

Other people seem quite the opposite. They can eat, drink and smoke their way to an early grave, with little awareness. We usually regard them as morally dissolute, but this may be unfair. They may simply have a poor instinct for health. They really can't feel what is good or bad for their bodies.

The difference between these two extremes is the degree of awareness. One person enjoys the taste of alcohol in his mouth and barely notices the consequences in his body. Another person can't drink without instantly registering its impact on his body and mind.

While one person has a low body awareness, the other has high body awareness and a good instinct for health. Fortunately, awareness can be learned, and meditation is one of the best ways to do this.

Remembered Wellness

The American psychologist Herbert Benson has for decades been investigating how certain people seem able to accelerate their healing processes. He says such people seem to have a strong instinct for health, which he calls "remembered wellness."[1]

He says that, deep within us, we know what it is like to feel completely healthy. He suggests that healing meditations activate that archetype of wholeness and deflect us from our usual focus on sickness. If our feeling for health is near the surface of consciousness, we will naturally behave in ways that amplify it.

So how do we recognize the feeling of health? First, it is good to realize that we all know what it is like to feel healthy. We may not be very healthy now, but we all have the memory of wellness.

For most of us, our childhood memories are drenched in the feeling of good health. When little, we have the abundant energy and resilience of growing things. We have confidence in our bodies and feel we can do anything. Even sickness is just a blip in the stream of health. Broken bones heal in no time. Illnesses flash by in a day or two. Even our exhaustion feels good and natural.

If we wish, we can activate the archetype of health through our imagination. We can recall the feeling of energy and confidence we had when young and healthy. We can reinforce the template of health and healing rather than succumbing to gloom.

A more direct approach is to recognize in detail the feeling of health and ill-health in the body. We instinctively recognize that the clenched jaw, the tight breathing, the anxious thought are unhealthy. Conversely, we realize that by releasing the jaw, the breath and thought, we become a little bit healthier.

As you meditate more, the healing process becomes very real and alive. Your body, or more literally the totality of sensations within it that we call the "energy-field," starts to loosen up. In time it feels soft, supple and fluid. It is like a stream of fine sensations—tingling, pulsing, warmth—both subtle and delightful, both calming and very alive. It resembles the feeling you get after aerobic exercise but is more refined and emotionally satisfying.

Health Is like Youth, Sickness Is like Old Age

We may no longer have the soft, strong, supple body of our youth but the memory alone can keep us healthy as we age. I spoke to a lady on her 79th birthday recently, and she said she really doesn't feel any different than she did when she was twenty.

Obviously her body is not what it was, but her mental attitude is keeping her young. Because she has a good instinct for remembered wellness, her body actually is young and healthy for her age. She still goes dancing, drives a car and is very active in the community.

Nonetheless, she is still 79, and her body was in much better shape half a century earlier. Most of us reach our peak of physical health and capacity in our early twenties. After that, it is all downhill. Each year our internal organs function a little less efficiently. In later years ailments like the flu, which a young body would throw off within days, can kill us. While you could say, "She is in excellent health for a 79-year-old," she is obviously much more vulnerable to sickness than a 20-year-old.

If we look at health solely in terms of being susceptible to illness, the healthiest are the young and the sickest are the old. As we age, we progress inexorably from health and vitality toward sickness and death. After the teenage years, the idea of perfect health is a dream. Good health is really a matter of aging slowly and delaying the inevitable.

The progression is inevitable, but its speed is up to us. Some people have reached the end of the line by forty. Others are still alive and kicking at ninety. If we can develop a good instinct for health, and can hold in mind the feeling of being young, we can slow the progression enormously.

So what is that "young" healthy feeling in the body? If our energy-field feels soft and flowing, we are in a healthy state. If it feels hard and stiff, it is tending towards sickness. It is easy to illustrate this by comparing children and old people.

In general, children are soft, supple, fluid and energetic. Old people, on the other hand, are hard, stiff, solid and sedentary. As we age and become less healthy, bones become stiff and brittle. Muscles lose their elasticity and range. We become stiff and limited in our movements. Once we could do cartwheels, but now it is even uncomfortable to run.

Infants are so soft their bones bend rather than break. Within the soft fluid bodies of babies in the womb, there are huge fluxings of sensation and activity. The softer the body, the more things move through.

The process of growth itself, which goes on for twenty or more years, is characterized by continual ongoing transformations of matter and energy. When young, we are drenched in the raw ingredients of good health.

As we grow older, we become more defended and we shut things out. We reduce our energy expenditure. We are less active and less emotionally enthusiastic about things. Rather than burning energy as young people do, we conserve it (and store it as fat!).

Staying Young as We Grow Old

It is up to us how quickly or slowly we age. If we keep our muscles supple, we keep them young. It helps enormously to use each part of the body regularly, and keep good aerobic energy flowing through the system. If we do this, we continue to feel alive and vital rather than stiff and hard, even if the years are piling up.

Fortunately, the body is enormously resilient. If it's not too late, you can turn the clock back a few years at least. After a huge health shock, people often realize they are heading to an early grave. If they then take their health seriously, within a few months or years they can recover much of the lost ground.

People at sixty can be healthier than they were at fifty. When younger, they may have been suffering a range of stress-induced ailments. As they get older and wiser, they know how to cope with pressure better, they eat and exercise consciously and they know how to enjoy themselves. They start to act and feel like younger people.

Our emotional well-being is even more important than exercise. 90% of the muscular tension we feel comes from worry and thinking, not from physical exertion. We age more from anxiety than from the passing years.

I am delighted to see how older people often grow younger. I am sure this is part of the wisdom of age. When people retire, they often lose the serious demeanor of their working life, and enjoy themselves more. As Bob Dylan said in a song, "But I was so much older then— I'm younger than that now."

Older people often grow into a healthy eccentricity. Less concerned about what people think of them, they express their emotions and thoughts more freely. By living more in the present and acting with the innate confidence of young people, they become young in spirit.

Older people often reclaim the emotional completeness of children. Their minds become supple, riding comfortably through the natural highs and lows of their thoughts and moods. They express more of the shadow side of their personality, rather than suppressing it. By sixty, we usually realize we will never be perfect or loved by everyone. So we give up the futile effort and do the intelligent thing: we relax and accept ourselves just as we are.

Is This Thought Good for Me?

Healing is rarely, if ever, like a surgical intervention that chops out the sickness and throws it in the garbage can. Our healing takes place through thousands of small incremental improvements. Little by little, you weed out the unhealthy thoughts, sensations and activities.

At any time you can ask yourself, "Is this thought (or activity, or sensation) healthy for me or not?" The simplest way to answer this is to read the body signs. If you find while considering an option that you are holding your breath, or if the muscles are starting to tense, it is probably unhealthy, no matter what the mind says.

Conversely, if you feel the body loosening and a sense of energy or life moving through you, it is probably healthy. It brings you energy rather than draining it.

If you are unsure, ask yourself, "If this thought or sensation was ten times stronger, would it feel good or bad for me?" Usually, you know immediately. Often the issue is not easy to resolve, however. You may know in your bones that your job or relationship is bad for you, but it may well have much that is good in it as well.

Frequently, you will find yourself glued to something harmful that takes time, sometimes years, to extract yourself from. But when you know the taste of health and you consciously pursue it, the route is clear and you are bound to get good results in time.

Loving Kindness

This Buddhist meditation stimulates that sense of warmth and affection we feel toward others when we are in a good mood. It has qualities of friendliness, acceptance, empathy and goodwill. It includes a sense of non-separation, as if you are "in touch" with yourself and others.

Imagine your heart opening like a flower, radiating soft pink light through your body. This is the light of loving kindness. You can amplify the effect by saying a word (such as "love" or "peace") as a silent chant, or the traditional Buddhist phrase, "May I be well and happy."

When you feel happy and content, share the feeling with others. One by one, imagine people you love. Hold them non-verbally in your heart for a few seconds each. Or send a beam of light from your heart to theirs. Or see them surrounded in a bubble of light. Be playful and enjoy the feeling in your body.

Gradually expand the range of your affection. Send it to acquaintances, animals, insects, people you have difficulty with, the city you live in, your country and the world. Don't get too heady. Return to yourself if the feeling fades.

If you know someone who is sick, hold them in your mind with affection, wishing them well. If you like, send white light to the parts of their body that feel as if they need it.

❀

EIGHTEEN

Detachment and Awareness

❀

Disarming the Stress Response Rapidly

We are designed to respond rapidly to a perceived threat. Ideally the stress response flares up rapidly and fades away when no longer needed. We suffer from stress only when we stay aroused for too long, in the misguided belief that it will help.

When we respond to a stressor, the initial stimulus is processed by the hypothalamus, which activates both the emotional brain (the limbic system) and the thinking brain (the neo-cortex). The emotional brain triggers an instinctive response within milliseconds while the thinking brain takes longer to process the data. So we have a rapid but crude arousal, followed by a cooler appraisal and a gradual return to homeostasis.

The instinctive response is rapid because the thinking brain processes things too slowly for safety. And we usually overreact, because this is safer than underreacting. A mouse that leaps ten feet from a snake-like rustle in the grass is more likely to survive than one that leaps one foot.

So our response is likely to be extreme until we get the rational report from the neo-cortex. The initial response is far too quick to change. Our ability to restore balance depends on how we manage our emotions thereafter. If we relax too slowly or inadequately, we suffer from chronic stress and die young.

Every day we respond to thousands of different stimuli. We notice many of them—a shower of rain, a sharp word, a song on the radio, a headache, a passing memory—but we rarely notice our response. If we were completely aware, we could respond appropriately to all of them—enjoying the good, feeling the bad, not taking anything too personally.

Alternatively, we could let everything niggle us and extend our time in the stress zone indefinitely. If we respond with an excess of negativity, our bodies and our health will respond as if we have been to hell and back. It is our choice. Do we hate the freeway traffic and the supermarket? Or do we make the best of the situation and still find moments of enjoyment amid the busyness?

Staying Stuck: Blaming the Stimuli

Emotions are impelling us to do something, and we often displace that tension inappropriately. If we can't yell at the boss, we complain about the weather. If we feel sad and lonely, we reach for food or a beer or the TV remote. We prefer to fixate on the outer stimuli such as a work situation or a broken leg rather than notice the emotion itself. Consequently, emotions can be hard to see with clarity.

It is easy to see the stimuli. It is much harder to acknowledge the depth and subtlety of our responses. Once we see them, however, we are less inclined to feed them and they tend to change of their own accord.

With age, we learn to work through difficulties with people, cut down on self-destructive activities, and manage our moods better. However, our emotional health depends just as much on the thousands of small responses each day as on the two or three big ones. This is where meditation and self-awareness become invaluable.

Meditation Is Not an Escape

Many people try to use meditation as an escape from their mental pain. They think of it as a blank state, free of all pain and distractions —something like a perfect holiday or one step short of the oblivion of sleep.

This state is like a little escape from one's usual thoughts and feelings and everyday life. Even if you attain it, it has its disadvantages. Coming out of it can be a shock. If our only way to cope with life is to escape, we will always be caught flat-footed when reality hits us in the face again.

Meditation is much more useful than this slightly hypnotic state of escape. It takes you into the middle ground between denying a feeling or surrendering to it. If we can watch our thoughts and feelings with detachment, we are no longer at their mercy and don't have to battle them. The pain remains but we don't amplify it. We call this the art of "just watching," or "noticing with detachment," or "being an observer" or "bare awareness."

So if you are stressing out, you don't have to go away and meditate. You just switch to watching mode on the spot. You "just watch" the body signs: agitation, headache, stiff breathing. You "just watch" the quality of your thinking: extreme, speedy, unbalanced. You also notice your emotional tone: angry, frustrated, hurt.

By just watching, you step back from the need to do anything, which immediately extracts you from the battle. You gain perspective and the landscape becomes clearer. Being a spectator requires far less energy than trying to sort things out. You relax even though the problems don't go away.

Being able to "just watch" any thought or feeling with detachment is much more valuable than temporarily escaping them. The escape is always brief—rarely more than a few minutes long—and dependent on good circumstances. But the observer mind can operate anywhere, anytime, defusing your responses and keeping you close to homeostasis.

Detachment Is Not Indifference

People are occasionally worried "If I meditate and calm down, will I also become cold and unfeeling?" It is true that some people elevate non-feeling to a virtue. They meditate to enter a numb glazed-eyed state that insulates them from reality, and often complain that ordinary life with its messy passions is gross and unspiritual in contrast.

However, detachment can have quite another quality. Just because we escape the grip of a thought or feeling doesn't mean we turn our back on it. In fact, we can see it in its full glory, just as it is. "Just watching" has a quality of acceptance, and even love, about it. It takes things as they are, and gives them space to be.

An emotional response or a block-out, on the other hand, is often an attempt to manipulate the situation. Whether we like or dislike a thought, sensation or feeling, we usually try to do something with it to make ourselves feel better. Both desire and aversion have a restless anxiety about them that clouds the mind.

Paradoxically, if you can "just watch," you become freer in your emotional life. When I started to meditate years ago and became more at ease with myself, I felt less need to control my emotions. Meditation has made me more, not less, emotional.

Meditation Trains You to Be an Observer

We practice the art of "just watching" in virtually every meditation we do. Even the best of meditators can't keep his mind focused on his object to the exclusion of all else. You can't help but notice the pulsing of a headache, a conversation outside, a thought about work, a sense of fatigue or sadness, a memory or dream image, a small fly landing on your wrist.

When you are focusing on your object, you practice the art of escape. When you notice peripheral things, however, you are practicing the art of detachment. The mind naturally oscillates from one to the other.

A good meditator can watch literally anything that arises without being distracted by it. She watches the breath and notices the traffic simultaneously. A less skilled meditator may get annoyed by the sound of a car, or an obsessive thought, and feel it has interrupted his meditation. "If only there weren't any cars," he thinks, or "I'm too stirred up to meditate right now." And sure enough, another car passes or another thought arises.

Some things, such as the sound of passing traffic or a slight headache, are relatively easy to watch without reacting. Others, such as an insoluble problem or a sense of fatigue, are more difficult to cope with. Meditators learn over time how to "just watch" an ever-increasing range of stimuli without overreacting, which keeps their bodies that much closer to balance.

When you meditate, you notice both the stimuli (the traffic noise) and your response (annoyance). The little knots of physical and emotional tension that arise in meditation usually need to be acknowledged before they dissolve. Once you allow a painful thought, memory or sensation to surface, the release can be surprisingly quick. The moment you stop obsessing about a person or event, your facial muscles can soften, for example.

With each release comes a little flash of pleasure. It's usually quite brief, as something else takes its place in the mind, but these moments of freedom build and compound. You become more settled and the mind feels spacious and light. Unpleasant thoughts and sensations may not disappear—that's not the aim—but they become easier to live with.

As we go deeper in meditation, we develop immunity to the thoughts. When we are in that "wanting nothing, fearing nothing" state, the inner delight is much more attractive than our usual thoughts anyway. Because we are no longer interested in them, they can't touch us.

At this stage, strange to say, we may have many more thoughts and feelings than before, but they fly by rapidly, unable to land on our "non-stick" mind. We notice them almost as if they are happening to someone else. We realize our thoughts and feelings are not as important as they pretend to be. We don't have to process them. We have all had squillions of thoughts in our lifetime and yet, right now, all except one of them has vanished.

When the mind is this clear, what the Buddhists call "insight" can arise. Answers to problems often pop up, through lateral associations or images or gut feelings. You can even voluntarily investigate a thought, image, feeling or issue without becoming stuck to it.

What Does It Mean to "Just Watch"?

"Just watching" means you notice how you are responding to an unwanted sensation, thought, feeling or situation, and you can wind down quickly if your response is excessive. Here are some examples:

You realize, driving to work, that you are in an irritable mood. It's Tuesday and you wish it were Friday. You realize this mood has nothing to do with the outer world. You're just tired because you didn't sleep well last night. By "just watching" your irritability, you no longer project it onto your surroundings.

Your wife pushes your buttons. By "just seeing" her actions, you realize she wasn't deliberately trying to aggravate you. By "just seeing" your own reaction, you realize it reminds you of what went on between you and your mother, many years ago.

You feel exuberant and able to handle anything. You walk out of the café and the sky is brighter than ever. Then you "just watch" this feeling, and you realize "It's the caffeine rush." You realize you could easily become noisy and hyperactive for a few hours, and burn out by nightfall.

That familiar deep pain in your spine starts up. You notice the accompanying emotions of despair and helplessness. By "just watching" them, you remember that you are not helpless. You know what to do to manage the pain, and you know it will go in time. You can acknowledge the pain without letting the despair amplify it.

❀

Naming the Problems

This is an emergency or "first aid" meditation, if you find you are riled up during the day. When you realize your thinking is completely unproductive, just stop and ask yourself "What is this?"

You can answer by naming both the stimuli and your response. If you are obsessing about what Mary has done to you, you say "Mary."

Then you name your reaction: "irritation" or "disappointment." It is traditional to name two or three times, to help you stand back from it. If you see your reaction clearly, it becomes less extreme and automatic.

You can take this a stage further by finding a metaphor to fully illuminate the feeling. If you ask "What is this like?" an appropriate image often pops up in the mind. You may feel like a clapped-out car, or a threadbare sheet, or a hunted mouse. Images allow you to "just see" your feeling more accurately than words. (See Chapter 21 for more about this.)

✵

NINETEEN

What about Positive Thinking?

✵

For many people, positive thinking has almost as bad a reputation as Political Correctness. People who are seriously ill can be afflicted by well-meaning friends who exhort them to "Think positive. Don't give up the fight."

This seems such a blithe and superficial approach to the challenges of life. What does positive thinking mean when you are vomiting into a bucket? What does "fighting it" mean, when you are so wasted that people have to bathe and feed you? Is it really possible to change your health just by changing the way you talk to yourself?

Recently a lady phoned me in a panic. "I've got cancer!" she said. "I know I can't afford to have any negative thoughts. How can I shut them out?" It would have been easier for her to climb Mt Everest. It is not healthy to panic, but it is also unhealthy to deny that anything is wrong.

Nonetheless, positive thinking (hereafter referred to as PT) has at least a grain of truth within it. People who whine and complain a lot are usually not happy people, and their faces and bodies testify to this. Conversely, people who have an intelligent, well-balanced optimism often seem to get along well in life.

PT can help you stay focused on your goals, or help you keep the big picture in mind. It can give you a more balanced view of your situation if you are getting dragged down by negativities. Most of us can use some positive thinking in moderation.

However, moderation is a word that rarely seems to apply to PT. Its keenest exponents tend to have a fanatical and irrational belief in the power of the mind. While most kinds of meditation are relatively simple and clear, PT often involves some extreme assumptions. Let us first look at some of the pitfalls associated with it before looking at its strengths.

The Negative Side of Positive Thinking

PT can have an unsavory moral logic. If positive thinking can make you healthy, then obviously your negative thinking made you sick in the first place. In other words, sickness and misfortune are your own fault.

Historically, the clergy have often argued that disease is God's way of punishing the sinful. Even nowadays a sick person can be scapegoated by his friends. "Well, he brought it on himself. . . ." I've heard New Age people say "We shouldn't help people suffering from famine because it is their karma" (with the implication that they deserve it).

The founders of PT were religious leaders. The Jesuit St. Ignatius described the method as "an exercise of the will" to make yourself a better person, and fight the evil within. Similarly, the tenet that thoughts make you physically healthy or sick is a fundamental idea of Christian Science. The term "positive thinking" was invented by a clergyman, Norman Vincent Peale.

With the declining influence of religion, you are now encouraged to "believe in yourself" rather than in God. However, PT is still more of a religious belief than a psychological theory.

PT has an almost pre-Freudian, 19th-century theory of consciousness. It assumes we can impose conscious control on our thoughts, behavior and moods, and on the outer world as well, if our will is strong enough. However, anyone who looks knows that these things have lives of their own. The mind is too complex and clever for the ego to rule with an iron rod.

PT easily overlaps into escapism and denial. If you always try to be bright and happy, you have to suppress feelings of sadness, even when they are perfectly appropriate. This creates tension, not a sense of well-being. Good thoughts have to be continually sustained, like pedaling a bicycle, or they topple over.

Finally, positive thinking is still a kind of thinking, which is what makes us anxious in the first place. We actually have to let go of thoughts, or at least stop trying to direct them, if we want to relax deeply. While meditation is usually a simple and clear practice, PT can involve elements of striving, self-talk, faith, hypnosis, magic, moral imperatives and an extreme theory of consciousness. It can seem like a quagmire.

Three Ways of Seeing the World

Is it really possible to change your life by changing the way you talk to yourself? Most people can't, but a few can. For that minority, positive thinking can be an excellent tool.

We tend to fall into three broad types, depending on how we experience reality. We "think about," "see" or "feel" what is happening to us. We understand things through words (verbal types) or think in pictures (visual types), or sense things through our bodies and feelings (kinesthetic types).

In meditation, we usually get the best results using techniques that suit our temperament. Verbal types like to use words. Visual types like to use imagery. People who are more in touch with their bodies and non-verbal feelings will thrive on body-based meditations.

Verbal types often find body-based meditations quite boring. For them, words are where the action is, and everything else is secondary. For kinesthetic and visual types, however, words do not carry much weight. Their sense of reality resides in their bodies, feelings or images.

To such people, words seem like a superficial gloss over this deeper sense of being.

Verbal types often seem quite in control of their lives because they can articulate what is happening for them. In many ways, they live in their words and their heads. Kinesthetic types, in contrast, tend to do things because it feels right, without being able to say why.

Visualization and PT often try to exclude the kinesthetic sense. They aim to take you to some beautiful place or "spiritual" plane, away from the hard realities of the moment. PT involves an almost Platonic belief that thought is more pure and real than anything else.

Is positive thinking really a meditation practice?

Because words seem like the ultimate reality to some people, they get very good at using them. I have heard of one religious teacher who claimed to have read and reviewed 30,000 books for his followers. This is obviously a man who lives, eats and breathes words.

For strongly verbal types, nothing really exists until it can be grasped in words. They acknowledge sensation and feeling only when these have been translated into language. This means they understand the world primarily as a verbal construction. Consequently, by changing their words they really can change their reality.

Norman Vincent Peale's typical positive thinker is the self-made entrepreneur. It goes back to that turn-of-the-20th-century belief that any poor immigrant could arrive at Manhattan Island and become a millionaire, if he believed in himself. Since natural positive thinkers are verbal types, they talk themselves up when their spirits are down and boost themselves when things are going well. PT is more of a character trait than a technique.

When positive thinkers meditate, they tend to relax and reflect on what they want to achieve. This contemplative thinking is different from meditation in the Eastern sense, which usually aims to extract you from thinking. Positive thinkers usually cultivate a habit of useful self-talk that sustains and inspires them. Relaxation and clarity of mind are lower priorities.

Keeping the Purpose in Mind

Most of us are not strong verbal types, so we should use PT with more modest expectations. If we are sick, for example, we can lose the big picture and start to feel as though our regimen of pills, treatment, exercise or special foods is all a waste of time. PT can remind you what it's all for, the way a parent encourages a despondent child.

You can say, as you undergo chemotherapy, "This is poisoning the cancer cells and making my tumor shrink." This is more useful than saying, "This is making me sick. I hate it!"

In the same way, you could have a stock phrase to say for each important thing you do. For example, "This exercise is increasing my aerobic capacity and flushing the rubbish out of my veins." Or, "These pills are feeding the cells and boosting my immune system." Or, "These fruit juices are filling my body with live, healthy energy." You can use PT as a way of acknowledging what is good for you.

You can also use affirmations to enhance the good moods that arise during the day. Often such states are so brief we miss them. When you notice a mood that is life-enhancing and lifts your spirits, acknowledge it fully.

Enjoy the mood and find a word or phrase to crystallize it. It could be an adjective: loving, playful, determined, peaceful. It could be a phrase or a whole sentence: "I eat well" or "People enjoy my company." Say the phrase a few times as a slow chant, to deepen the effect.

Affirmations to Enhance Mood

PT can add a positive emotional flavor to other kinds of meditation. Rather than trying to "create our own reality" through words, we can use words playfully, as a kind of sympathetic (or "pretend") magic to brighten our state of mind. If, for example, you focus on the breath while saying the word "Peace," it may well reinforce or evoke that feeling.

Positive thinking combines well with imagery. You could say the word "Love," while evoking an appropriate scene or situation. Imagery usually has a stronger effect than words alone. Picturing a peaceful scene, or imagining a loved one, is more likely to change your body chemistry than just saying the words.

If we use an affirmation, it is good to hold it lightly in consciousness and not think too much about it. In other words, we use it to set a mood rather than as an instruction or order. After a while, affirmations tend to become more chant-like. The intellectual content fades and the non-verbal feeling comes to the fore.

For this reason, short simple affirmations usually take you deeper than long ones. It is much easier to hold a single word than a four-line affirmation when you go into deep states.

Chanting, even to this quiet degree, takes many people into a light hypnotic state in which words or phrases can have unusual strength. You say the word "Peace" and suddenly you feel peaceful. The hypnotist says, "You are now deeply relaxed," and you are!

When we relax we are more suggestible. Our usual critical function goes into abeyance, and we unthinkingly go along with what is said. In this state, words really can trigger feeling. This works best for those who are natural hypnotic types.

PT to Restore Emotional Balance

It's not unhealthy to be afraid of death, or to be anxious about the future, or to feel your marriage may fail. If these reasonable thoughts didn't arise occasionally, you would really be in trouble. It's much healthier to be honest with yourself than to hope a positive fantasy will stave off disaster.

It is only when such thoughts are excessive that they become unhealthy. Positive Thinking in such cases means restoring a more balanced view. This is similar to the psychological practice called Cognitive Therapy.

PT from this perspective means seeing the good and bad just as they are and boosting the positive if necessary. Even talking with friends can serve this function of helping you see things more rationally. If you find yourself panicking about your breast cancer, PT or a friend can put it in perspective for you. You can say to yourself, "Yes, it was scary, but finally it was just a small lump. The doctor believes he got it all. I have every chance of living another forty years."

PT doesn't have to be a denial of the situation. You just say "I'll do the best I can." You don't have to believe the pills or the treatment are going to work. You just have to say, "I'll give it a good go."

If you are seriously ill, you don't have to pretend nothing is wrong. If you want to collapse and cry, do it. It is healthier to let out this natural emotion than to suppress it. Only the blocked or exaggerated emotions maintain tension in the body.

PT and Terminal Illness

Finally, it is positive to accept the possibility of an early death. Dying is a natural process, and clinging desperately to a life that is fading can only increase the misery.

We frequently hear of people who outlived their "death sentence" from the doctor. It may seem as if their belief in themselves made them pull through. However, the doctors still weren't wrong. Their estimates are based on average life expectancies, and there will always be people at the extremes.

The doctors' estimates of the time of death are right 90% of the time, according to a recent study. The patients' estimates, on the other hand, are overly optimistic. Ninety percent of them think they will live longer than they actually do. I have seen people refuse to believe they are dying, even on the day of their death.

This kind of positive thinking can lead to a lot of unnecessary pain. Patients and their families insist the doctors do everything that might help. This means terminally ill people often undergo debilitating treatment that the doctors know will be useless. Instead of dying in a natural process, they suffer the added pain of unnecessary operations and drugs.

Affirmations

Use affirmations to set a mood rather than to stimulate thought. Don't be forceful. You are not giving orders. You could use an affirmation such as Peace, or Relax, or Be still, or Let it go, or Love. Or you could say any word or phrase, however strange, if it gives you a good feeling. Even a line from a song will do.

First, relax your body and breathing as usual. Now say an affirmation in time with the breath. Say the words as a silent chant and allow the chantlike quality to relax you. Add in a visualization if you like and enjoy the feeling in your body.

TWENTY

How to Meditate on an Illness

❋

People often want to target their illness directly. For example, they ask me, "How can I meditate on my cancer?" When they consult with me, however, I first look at the general ways they can relax and improve their quality of life. The fundamentals need to be attended to first. Let me remind you of all the ways meditation helps when you are ill.

The healing and repair mechanisms of the body work best when you are either relaxed during the day or asleep. They largely switch off when you are stressed or active. Therefore any meditation that restores you to homeostasis will help you. It doesn't have to be tailored to your particular illness.

The walking and "spot-meditations" that slow you down and enhance sensory pleasure will keep you close to homeostasis throughout the day. They are an excellent, even essential, complement to formal sitting meditation. It is much better to be fairly relaxed for several hours of the day than to depend on a few minutes of formal meditation to do the work.

The body-scanning practices of Chapter 7 are the healing meditations par excellence. To put it simply, the more you feel your "energy-field" in all its subtle detail, the more you nourish the body and strip out the physical and emotional negativities lodged within it.

Meditations based on "just watching" give you the detachment to clearly see what is happening to you. This enables you to respond in a balanced and considered way, rather than lurching from one apparent crisis to another.

Meditations on pain and on the negatives (Chapter 21) help you tolerate what you can't necessarily change, and defuse their power to irritate you. Meditations on the positives raise your spirits and remind you how beautiful life can be, despite the problems.

Once meditation becomes a modus operandi, you realize how many of the useful things you do can be done meditatively. Instead of thinking of your exercise in mechanical terms, you see it as a lovely opportunity to give the body pleasure and to relax the mind. By "just doing what you are doing," you do things better and enjoy them more.

Meditating Specifically on Your Illness

There is more you can do. You can make the illness your meditation object. For example, a person with cancer may visualize her tumor as a mass of small black crabs and imagine her killer T-cells and macrophages and chemotherapy as white knights in shining armor attacking them. Let me explain why this can be helpful.

First, she feels she is able to do something about her cancer. Psychologists have found this is a much healthier state of mind than feeling like a helpless victim.[1] Second, she is focusing on her cancer without fear (and fear can be just as deadly as cancer). She doesn't have to run from it in terror and be reluctant to even say the word. She is reminding herself she has powerful allies in her immune system and in her treatment.

Third, she is psychologically adjusting to the reality of her illness. Sickness typically comes like a bolt out of the blue, or crawls slowly from the darkness. It is all the more oppressive because it carries the fear of the unknown. By catching it in images, however, she is getting a handle on it. Instead of a mood of overwhelming dread, she can now hold it in a picture and see it with some detachment.

For these reasons alone, visualizing is likely to reduce her anxiety about her cancer. This will have excellent effects on the immune system and will help her entire body function better. But the benefits of such an exercise go further than this.

Awareness Heals

It is an axiom in meditation that awareness heals. Once you see a physical or emotional tension clearly, it starts to release. The clarity of mind is the secret ingredient. If you can see and accept what is happening without trying to change it, it starts to change. Once a problem is clearly acknowledged, be it a tight jaw or a sense of frustration, our non-verbal healing instincts start to work on it.

We assume we notice things clearly, but typically our minds just skim over the surface. For example, we may know we have cancer but dare not look too deeply at the repercussions of this. Consciousness (part of the mind that "sees") acts on a problem the way sunlight melts ice, and the more conscious we become, the better.

By focusing on an illness, whether we use a visualization or not, we are consciously acknowledging it. Focusing on a part of the body we may have neglected or never noticed is like flooding it with light. We start to sense or see it with increasing detail. We may feel the fine play of sensation in that place, or "see" it in our imagination, or both. This is the opposite of trying to suppress a feeling. I call it "allowing the body to speak." The conscious mind illuminates and "tags" the area, letting the deeper mind transform it.

Let's say the illness is cancer. While meditating, the subtle play of sensations around a tumor usually seems to change for the better. As the mind goes into microscopic detail, you feel something happening and it usually feels good. It can require courage as the subtle negatives are stirred to the surface. At this level, emotional and physical sensations (and images) are almost indistinguishable. The effect of consciousness flooding that part of the body is quite magical (and I apologize for not being able to explain it better).

There is another way to understand this. When we focus on an area we increase the blood supply to that place temporarily. This is a very real effect. If you attach a little thermometer to a finger and focus on it, the temperature will rise. When people say they are "giving energy" to that place, they are literally correct. The metabolic and immune system activity, and the flow of nutrients, all increase.

The effect is subtle but very encouraging to a meditator. It's lovely to feel a bundle of tight sensations gradually loosening as you focus on them. We may wonder if this practice works because of the physiological changes or because of the good emotional tone it evokes. I suspect it is a feedback loop: as the sensations feel better the mind feels good, which loosens up the body more, and so on. Hands-on healing may have a similar effect.

Developing a Healing Meditation

If you have a serious illness, it is good to develop a personal way of meditating on it. Firstly, it has to feel right for you and, secondly, it should work on both the emotional and physical levels.

Many of these meditations involve imagination. Only about a quarter of the population gets clear pictures when they visualize. Most of us don't visualize as well as we think we ought to, but it doesn't actually matter. It is enough to get a feeling or mood for the body chemistry to change.

❋

Visualizations for Healing

PURE AWARENESS

This is the simplest and probably the strongest practice of all. You simply focus on the site of your illness and allow all the physical and emotional sensations to emerge. Remember that awareness heals. If you wish, you can imagine consciousness as a light that illuminates all the dark and hidden corners of your disease. Ideally, your attention should be curious and exploratory, like a child exploring the delicate structure of a living insect. A clear mind has no fear or anger. It is non-judgmental and is quite happy to "just see" what is there. Within a few minutes, you notice your mind is relaxing and the sensations and subtle emotions are changing, without you having to do anything.

It can be useful to find out what your illness looks like. Then when you focus on it, you have some idea of the appearance of the tissues and organs, and the cells of the immune system. Use photographs and X-rays to enhance your awareness. These prompts can help you feel or "see" in more detail than you would otherwise.

NON-CONFLICT VISUALIZATION

At the cellular level, healing really is a battle, but you don't have to see it this way. You can imagine washing the illness with light, or love, or nectar, or a healing color. If your nature is more tactile, you can imagine massaging or caressing the injured tissue. You could ask the body, "What color do you want?" and imagine that color flowing through you. You could play music or say a mantra and imagine the gentle vibrations of the sound harmonizing the energies in your cells. Don't get too busy or try to make things happen. Have a good time, and let the body relax.

VISUALIZING THE BATTLE

Find some way of imagining the immune system at war with your illness. You can do this in a general way. For example, you may imagine the body being flooded with white light. (See the "White Light" meditation in Chapter 7.) Or you could see a laser light hitting the diseased cells.

However, you could be more precise and get to know exactly what macrophages, killer T-cells, helper cells, white blood cells and antibodies actually look like. Photographs and diagrams are readily available in books. See the hot-spots of the battle, and also imagine how the whole military campaign is working. In fact, the supply lines go right back to the processes of digestion and respiration. As you explore this you may, like a good general, notice what is lacking and what needs support.

IMAGING THE ILLNESS

Rather than seeing your illness much as it is, you could evoke an image that crystallizes it. If you see it as a smoldering fire, or as an invasion of parasitic worms, or as a crumbling castle, or as a poisonous swamp, you reveal to yourself how you are responding emotionally to your illness.

The more vividly you can feel or see your illness, the more rapidly it changes. This process can be augmented by drawing or painting the illness, or writing a description of it in words. By identifying the emotional complex accompanying the illness, you are disarming it at its core.

If you can capture the illness in an image, you know exactly what the target is, both emotionally and physically. Thus, you can imagine the healing forces that directly combat it. You have the attack troops— knights in white armor, or swat teams, or guerrilla fighters. You also have the arsenal, from pitchforks and hatchets to poison and nuclear bombs, and the diplomats, peacemakers and strategists working at the edges to bring hostilities to an end.

Although the healing process really is a war with billions of corpses, these visualizations are best done in a playful or even childlike fashion. It is best to relax almost to the point of sleep by using any ordinary practice, and then do the visualizing in a dreamlike stress-free mood. If you start visualizing before you relax adequately, the battle scenarios will only increase your anxiety and tension. Remember that the bottom line in any meditation is to relax the body!

A HEALING SANCTUARY

In this meditation, you go the whole hog. You imagine everything, real and fantastic, that would help you heal.

First, you evoke what would be the perfect place of healing for you (if only you could get away from the office!). It could be a place from childhood or a past vacation, or it could be purely imaginative: a shrine, a health spa, a crystal palace or a Chinese temple in the mountains.

Imagine roaming through it, enjoying the atmosphere and adding all the detail you want. Notice exactly what you want to do and hear and eat and see in order to nourish your soul. Be as sensual as possible. Feel the smooth edge and moist texture of a single leaf. Savor the song of a particular bird. Visualizations like this act like a hologram. Any single detail that catches your imagination will be as good as the whole picture.

Now meet your team of healers. They could be "real" people, such as the doctor you would really like to have, plus a naturopath or a physiotherapist or a masseur. Or the team might include archetypal beings such as a wise old woman, an herbalist, a Chinese doctor, a saint or a god ....

Talk with them and get intelligent answers. Imagine these beings can enter directly into your body and work at the micro-levels within you. The aromatherapist massages healing scents and oils into the tissues. The surgeon cuts out damaged flesh. The saint transforms the energy-field. When they are finished, ask their advice.

Now rest and recuperate in that beautiful place. Feel you have all the time in the world. Imagine doing anything—writing, hiking, singing, yoga, sleeping or just being—that could help you heal. Indulge and enjoy!

✸

TWENTY-ONE

Facing the Negatives, Enhancing the Positives

✸

Every day we are subjected to hundreds of unpleasant events. They can be big or small, physical or mental. A headache brings us down just as much as trouble at work. They may come as a pattern of small irritating moments, such as a persistent cough, or as a one-time disaster, like a car accident.

Collectively, we can call them "the negatives." By definition, a negative is anything that brings you down or dampens your *joie de vivre*. We can't avoid the pain they cause, but we can minimize their effects. With the right attitude, many will cease to be negatives at all.

The two fundamental skills of meditation—focusing and watching—help us disarm them. By focusing on a negative, we see it clearly instead of trying to escape it. We can identify it in all its detail, just as a doctor has to diagnose an illness before curing it. Additionally, by noticing it with dispassion, we abandon our usual kneejerk reaction to it. Our dislike of a negative can be worse for us than the negative itself.

Here are some small negatives we may face during the day. We wake with a foggy mind. The thought of getting up appalls us. We turn on the radio news and hear squabbling politicians. The shirt we thought was clean is in the laundry basket. We find we have run out of milk. The interpersonal dynamics in the kitchen leave much to be desired.

We leave home late and the traffic is worse than usual (then we realize it has been worse than usual for months!). The plant on the desk seems to be dying. By midday, you realize you strained your back while gardening on the weekend.

Throughout all of this there are positives as well. The shower woke us up, breakfast tasted good, the sky was lovely as we drove to work, and our work is going well. Our days are usually an alternation of good and bad moments.

At times, however, the negatives can really get on top of us. We are obviously suffering from stress if it seems too much to return that phone call or cook another meal. Our general health depends to a large degree on how we cope with these petty ongoing stressors.

A common response is anger and attack. Years ago, my dog jumped into the back of my truck. She caught her foot in the tray as she did so, twisting her whole leg painfully. I grabbed her and threw her out again, to untwist her. However, she was so blind with pain she bit a chunk out of my arm on the way. When we are suffering, we just lash out and hope for the best.

When we are stressed, we feel we have to fight continuously just to stay in control. But the enemy starts to invade the boundaries of our skin. We become afraid of our thoughts, our feelings, and the painful signals from our own body. If we have cancer, it may seem like our whole being is imploding into malignancy.

Anger comes in many flavors. The basic aversion can also express itself in resentment, fear, annoyance, bitterness, agitation, contempt, self-hatred and non-specific irritability. En masse, these will kill us just as efficiently as a heart attack.

Occasionally anger is appropriate, but if your problem is caring for a demented spouse, it will probably fail. Anger is an attempt to drive away or kill a negative. This is not a good way to deal with things that are going to stay around for years. If we can't kill the enemy, we have to find some healthy way of relating to him. Eventually, the only way is to make love, not war.

When the enemy invades the homeland (and any small negative does just that), all is not lost. It is time to give up the fighting and start negotiating. When this happens, you may find the enemy is not what you thought it was.

When Jews negotiate with Arabs, or Bosnians face Serbs, they can't help but notice they are talking to human beings, not demons. The enemy then becomes a person who suffers, laughs and sometimes thinks intelligently, just like us. Similarly, we don't need to demonize the negatives in our lives. We don't have to like them to arrange a truce with them.

Instead of firing shots at them from a distance, we agree to meet them (i.e., we focus on them). Then we listen to what they have to say (i.e., we watch them with detachment). Curiously enough, that is all we need to do to defuse the tension. In this way, you find you have signed an armistice that enables you both to demobilize your troops. Often a new and unexpected relationship starts to develop after that.

Acknowledging the Negatives

I often do a micro-meditation when I find myself overreacting to a mood, a sensation, a thought or a situation. I identify my unhelpful response and defuse it on the spot. Yet the negative is still a negative. It doesn't make us feel good. So how can we relate to it? The strategy goes somewhat as follows:

First, acknowledge its presence. Second, notice it in detail and let it express itself. Third, notice if your reaction is healthy or unhealthy. Are you relaxing into it, or putting on the battle armor?

For example, you see a letter from your ex-wife's lawyer in the mail. Even without opening it you feel really bad. The first stage is to acknowledge the presence of that feeling, rather than moving on to something else.

The second stage is to meditate on it. Avoiding the temptation to think about it, you simply notice how the negative is making you feel.

Your stomach and shoulders may sink. You feel the wind is taken out of your sails. It can help to "name" the emotional tone—despair or frustration or loss.

Finally, notice if your response is healthy or unhealthy. Are you relaxing into the feeling? In other words, are you letting it surface and release? Or are you stiffening against it and trying to drive it underground? Also notice if your response is excessive. You may well know that the letter is about some trivial matter that can be dealt with lightly.

This whole exercise may take less than twenty seconds. You let the pain surface, you feel its emotional resonance and respond rationally if you need to do anything. Then you get on with things, without carrying the ill-feeling into the rest of the day.

Catching the Feeling in an Image

We often dwell on a negative in ways designed to smother the actual feeling. I find images are an extremely useful way of illuminating the feeling and helping it out. Rather than trying to describe it in a word, I catch it in an image. I identify the issue, notice where I feel it in my body, and get an image that illustrates the feeling. I find that images (such as a bloody axe) are much more vivid and accurate than a word (such as "anger").

Once, after a phone conversation, I felt bad for no apparent reason, so I asked, "What is this?" The image came up immediately. It was as if I had eaten moldy fruitcake. It was so appropriate I had to laugh. The woman I was speaking to was a psychologist with enormous abilities (the cake), which were contaminated by her paranoia (the mold). By getting the image, I knew how I would instinctively respond to her in the future.

Often during the day I ask, "What is this?" and extract a feeling that is starting to trouble me. I may feel dry and stiff, like a dead branch. I may feel like a squashed tin can. I may feel effervescent like a fountain.

I find the image puts me deeply in touch with myself again. If it tells me I am tired, I start to pace myself. If I feel sad, I give the feeling space to trickle through during the next few minutes. If I find myself irritable or restless, I am careful not to spill it out onto other people.

I never try to fight off or eradicate the bad feeling. I try to give it space and a little love, so it can come forth in its own way. It is a part of me, and if I acknowledge it, the tension usually dissipates fairly quickly.

Formally Meditating on the Negatives

Negatives can be hard to avoid, so I often meditate directly on them. In other words, I make a certain negative my meditation object. This relaxes me by defusing a latent tension, and clears my mind of an obsession.

The instructions go:

1. Identify the negative
2. See where it is in the body
3. Get an image that illustrates it
4. Make the image as vivid as possible
5. Let it go, and cultivate an "antidote image"

Many years ago after I broke up from a longtime girlfriend, I felt so dreadful I could hardly bear the idea of her being in the same city. In meditation I had to face this, so I asked, "Where is this feeling in the body?" (That was easy. It was in the heart.)

Then I asked "What is it like?" Well, it was black and explosive. It was a floating World War II mine in a stormy sea. It looked mean. It was covered in barnacles and barbed wire. The knobs on it were hissing and spitting as well.

That was all I needed to do at that moment. I felt a great sense of relief. By catching it in an image, I could see it with detachment. It was still huge, but no longer overwhelming me. I checked as the weeks and months went by and it gradually shrank. After two years it was just a fleck of soot. After three years of avoiding my ex-girlfriend, we cautiously resumed a friendship.

Once the image is clear, you often feel a palpable release in the body. By objectifying it, you no longer feel so glued to it. Once you feel that release, you ideally let the negative go and shift your attention to other things.

Nonetheless, the negatives are sticky and not that easy to detach from. We like to continue poking around in the mess. Do we feel more alive if we are torturing ourselves?

It can help to focus on an "antidote image." This is an image that has a physical effect completely opposite from the negative images. If your negative is dark, heavy and dirty, you imagine something light and clean. If your negative image is a lead ball in the stomach, you imagine a downy feather floating in the clouds.

People often find the antidote is not so much an opposite as a modification of the negative. If their negative is a dirty twisted rag, they imagine untwisting it, cleaning it carefully and hanging it out to dry.

The aim is to change the physiological impact of the negative. One of my students was having trouble in her workplace, so she imagined making love to her boyfriend on the beach. This would certainly have changed her body chemistry!

This Meditation Can Go Wrong

This meditation is likely to come unstuck if you try to do it without getting an image. The image traps and contains the negative so it doesn't spill all over you. If you try to process the negative in words, you are much more likely to inflame the issue.

If you don't get images easily, you can prime the unconscious by asking, "If the feeling was in the body, where would it be? If it had a color, what color would it be? If it had a texture, would it be smooth or rough?" By the time you know the image is dark grey and rough, you can ask "rough like what?" And the image often arises at that point: rough like sandpaper (or carpet, or kiwifruit, or a brick . . .).

Once you have an image, you play with it like a child doing a drawing. You add on the bells and whistles to make it more graphic.

It is surprising how satisfying this is. By trapping an amorphous feeling into an image, you can have fun with it.

Finally, your problem may be a human being, but he or she can't be the image. The image represents your feeling, which is something quite different. If Peter makes you feel like garbage, then you get an image of garbage, not of Peter. This meditation works on our response, not on the stimulus, which is usually out of our control. This meditation is designed to change your body chemistry, not solve the outer problem—though understanding can arise as your reaction improves.

Enhancing the Positives

Imagination works because our bodies respond not to an event but to our perception of it. If we are thinking anxiously about a past event, our bodies will respond as if it is still happening. We may be trying to have a nice time on the weekend, but if we can't stop thinking about work, our bodies will respond as if it is still Tuesday morning.

Conversely, we may be in a hospital bed, but if we are going over pleasant memories of our home in the country, our bodies will assume that is where we are. We may still be in physical pain, but our mind is in another place, de-stressing.

When we meditate, we can choose where to direct our mind and what to put in the background. This is particularly good when under pressure. One of the best ways of doing this is through images.

Images are more sensual than words. Both carry meaning and feeling but images tend to be more stable and emotionally rich than words. Good thoughts require continual effort to maintain and often lack flavor.

Images do not need to be exclusively visual. They can come via any sense. You can recall a sound image—a piece of music for example—or a flavor, just as much as a picture. You can imagine things through any sense—sight, sound, smell, taste or touch. Or an image may start as a picture and trigger off other sense associations, emotions and a body response.

For example, you "see" a favorite dog. You realize the senses of touch, smell and hearing are also involved. Then you feel affectionate and your body relaxes. The full spectrum of an image includes emotion and a body response as well as sensation.

I generally like my images fresh. Rather than constructing a certain scene in my mind and always returning to it, I prefer to pluck something from recent memory. The chapter on "Smart Sensuality" (Chapter 16) gives examples of ways to do this.

I also use images that come up spontaneously. In meditation, the unconscious mind often throws up memories or dream images. When this happens, I don't "go with the flow." I choose just one of these images and meditate on it. I observe color, shape, texture and emotional resonance, just as I would with any visual object. I enhance the sensuality of the image, and I don't let myself get distracted into thinking about what it means.

Similarly, when a good feeling happens in a meditation, I enhance it by catching it in an image. Just as I do with a negative, I ask, "What is this like?" It could be like a quiet flowing stream. It could be like the moon rising on an autumn night. It could be like a bubble of pink light around the body.

There are traditional images that describe some of the good feeling one gets in meditation. You may feel as if your body is like a flower in full bloom. Or that nectar is flowing down through the body, or that a pale fire is rising up the spinal column.

You don't have to use traditional images, however. It is enough to remember some good feeling, get an image that illustrates it and enjoy it. This is still a formal meditation practice. You choose an object that just happens to be an imaginary one and become absorbed with it. You notice when the mind wanders and bring it back. You periodically check your body, to see if you are actually relaxing and not just having a think-fest.

The feeling of love can be evoked in many different ways. You may, for example, bring to mind a conversation with a friend. It may not have been intense, but possibly there was a feeling of gentle appreciation between you. So you ask yourself, "What is this like?" and get an image.

Possibly it is like a sheet of handmade paper, or the note of a flute, or the humming of bees on a summer afternoon. If you can hold the feeling in an image, it will relax you more deeply than just thinking about your friend.

Similarly you could imagine playing with your cat, or seeing your grandchild, or the unspoken camaraderie of a sports game. Meditating on these feelings can make a huge difference to your biochemistry and sense of well-being.

Good Feeling Is Naturally Unstable

It is useful to remember that no feeling stays for long. The word emotion means "moving out," and it is the nature of feelings to be constantly changing.

For this reason it is best to amplify a feeling when it is present, but not to hold on to it when it fades. The nature of imagination exercises should be light and playful. If we try to grimly construct or sustain an image, it will make us tense and frustrated. Their very nature is fluid.

While healthy sensations tend to move and change, unhealthy sensations tend to feel hard and stuck. This also applies to emotions. An unhealthy emotion, because of its stuck, unexpressed nature, can stay around for days. This makes it easy to crystallize into an image and to meditate on.

Healthy emotions, however, are continually fluid and changing. They also tend to lack the obsessive charge of a negative, which makes them more difficult to hold in an image. They have a lighter and more expansive quality.

For this reason, it is often best not to base a meditation solely on an image or feeling. Images usually work best as an overlay to something more stable, such as the breath or the body or a repeated phrase. When the images start to fade, you don't have to pump them up again.

You just return to home base and wait. Images and feeling can be very useful, but they can take a lot of effort to sustain on their own.

❋

Place of Power

Some places, because of their natural beauty or the memories associated with them, give us energy and lift our spirits. It is not hard to return to them in imagination, particularly when we really need a break from what is happening around us.

Imagine a place and walk into it. It may be somewhere from your past or a pure fantasy. Go slowly and enjoy sight, sound, smell and texture. Don't try to paint the full picture. Go for the small detail instead: the touch of a stone wall, the steam rising from a cup of tea, the moss that grows on the bark of the old tree ....

❈

TWENTY-TWO

Cancer and Serious Illness

❈

In this chapter I talk about serious, chronic and debilitating sicknesses, including those that turn out to be terminal. Since cancer can fit into all of these categories, I use it as a representative example of the other serious illnesses as well.

When we first become ill, we tend to think of it mainly as a medical problem. We look at all the things the doctors can do and we can do, mainly in terms of repairing our bodies.

Soon we realize it can't be contained in this way. Its effects spread far beyond our bodies. The weekly schedule is rearranged. You may change patterns of diet, exercise, work and recreation. Your friends, family and workmates respond to you differently when they hear you have cancer. Your inner sense of body and self have to adjust to the presence of a malignancy inside you.

Illness is largely a solitary journey into a land of new sensations and feelings, new events, dangers and decisions. You can inform yourself and get all the advice you want from friends and professionals, but once you are fully there, the landscape often looks nothing like the map. And it is happening to no one else but you.

Meditation will help your whole body function well so it can better combat the cancer. However, meditation is equally valuable in dealing with the psychological issues. Despair, pain and confusion can defeat you just as much as a malignant growth can. Confidence, clarity of mind and intelligent management of your situation can heal you just as well as chemotherapy.

Meditation can help spare you from being overwhelmed by your illness. You don't need to make cancer such an integral part of your personality that you think of yourself as "a cancer sufferer," tempting as that may be.

It is said that grieving for a dead spouse usually takes a year or two at best. And yet the widow is not grieving all that time. She can be puttering around her beloved garden with the birds, the flowers, the wind and the weeds, and suddenly realize she is completely happy and has actually forgotten him for a few minutes at least. If this happens only a week after the funeral, she may feel quite embarrassed and hope that no one notices.

But this is what a normal mind is like. For inner health and a sense of well-being, it seeks out pleasure, even in the worst of situations. Even if we are terminally ill, there can be many hours when we feel quite okay—even radiantly happy. This can be quite a shock for people who visit you with long faces.

When one woman realized she might only have a year to live, it made her fully awake. "As soon as I was diagnosed with cancer, the world became brighter. It was like someone had turned the lights on."

If she were a meditator, she could ride that moment of illumination and enhance its effect. Much of her day of course would still be occupied by the mundane. But meditation, as the art of entering the present moment, would enable her to savor those bright moments more and more.

A Chance to Think Deeply

Illness often gives one the opportunity to rest and contemplate the bigger issues in life. Many people find catching the flu gives them the excuse they need to step off the treadmill for a day, stay at home and take stock of themselves.

When you are seriously ill, people usually don't expect you to earn a living. You have time to think at last! Even under these circumstances, the chance to contemplate your life can be a great pleasure. Sickness can give you the sabbatical or retirement you have wanted for so long.

Sickness can lead to a richer, more intuitive kind of thinking. It becomes blindingly obvious what is important and what is not. A man with AIDS said, "As I walked out of the doctor's office, my thoughts about redesigning the kitchen vanished forever."

Ideally in meditation you don't actively think. You aim to create a space in which inner wisdom can arise. In Buddhism, this is called "insight." In a flash, you understand the situation and you know what to do.

Insight has many dimensions. Insight can be about big or small matters, or it can be an ongoing stream of clear, inspired thinking. Often it has a clean-up function, unraveling the gritty knots of emotional pain and dispelling the confusion. At other times, it elevates the "just watching" quality of meditation into an almost godlike perspective. This can have a philosophic or spiritual quality which is healing in itself.

Meditation can refine the introspection that often occurs with illness. Our usual verbal thinking can easily incline toward fantasy and self-deception. Meditation, however, as does illness in general, grounds your thinking and understanding in the body. In other words, you think with your whole body, not just your head.

A Clear, Balanced Mind

Equally valuable is the ability to "just watch" the ramifications of your illness. If you meditate regularly, your mind will be clearer and better able to steer you through the options. New things are continually coming into the equation. If you notice, "Oh! this is happening now," you can meet new circumstances intelligently, even if you haven't had to deal with them before.

If a diagnosis of cancer is suddenly thrown into your life, how are you going to respond? By dropping everything and plunging into it? Or by trying to lead as normal a life as possible, even if that seems to be part of the problem?

You could go into the extremes of panic or denial. While neither is useful, it can be good to oscillate somewhat between them. It is natural and healthy to have times of sadness and despair, and it is good to enjoy the times you feel just fine despite the diagnosis.

Meditation helps maintain your emotional as well as physical homeostasis. When you first hear that your cancer diagnosis is confirmed, what do you do with this huge dark secret? You've never been in this situation before. If you're a meditator, you will instinctively know, "This is a time to meditate."

You relax and settle into your body as well as you can. Your mind may be frantic, but at least you can drop the physical agitation that came from driving and running around all day. You can let the breathing soften and sigh, and feel your body shift from arousal towards resting mode.

Ideally, you "just watch" the thoughts and feelings racing through your mind. "I hate this! This can't be happening to me. I feel just fine! What did I do wrong? Shall I tell people at work? I can't tell my kids. I'll quit work and do all the alternative therapy things. I can't bear to think about it. I'll tell the doctors to just do everything they want. Shit! Maybe I'll die. I might even lose my hair. I'm not going downhill the way Elaine did. God, I feel tired. I want to go to sleep and forget all about it."

Getting a cancer diagnosis can be like falling in love. The mind is likely to be in turmoil for days or weeks until everything is factored in, one change after the other, and you find the point of balance in the new situation. It is like sailing a small boat in a hurricane. Calm weather may be nowhere in sight, but anything that keeps you upright is invaluable.

You'll face many new options, inner and outer. If you don't cope with them well, you'll feel stressed and over-burdened. This will affect your health just as much as the illness itself. On the other hand, if you manage your changing situation to your own satisfaction, your sense of well-being will be enhanced enormously. Meditation is as likely to help cure cancer by fostering a healthy state of mind as it is by stimulating the self-healing mechanisms of the body.

Making Your Own Choices

How you respond to an illness is as much a reflection of your personality as it is of anything else. Some people really discover their true identity when they get seriously ill. Doctors, friends and family give us clear cues on how they expect us to behave. But do we really want to be told what to do while we are ill, in much the same way that Mommy decided what we would wear to school?

Research indicates it is important to maintain a sense of being in control of your treatment. The alternative—letting people do what they want with you—can be quite unhealthy for you. When rats are trained into "learned helplessness," they suffer high stress hormone levels and suppressed immune function. The result is very similar in humans who are depressed or lonely. The sense of being in control, even if it is an illusion, leads to a healthier physiological environment than just giving up.[1]

When faced with an option, do you decide, "They all seem to want me to have the operation, so I'll do it to make them happy. They're doing so much for me anyway." Or do you decide to wait another week or two until you really know what you want?

Hundreds of times in the course of an illness, you'll be faced with choices about how to act. If you are a meditator you will wait for the inner signals to tell you what to do. The Buddhists say that every single thought (and any ensuing action) has either a healthy or an unhealthy result. Meditators have a way of telling which is which that most people don't have. They can read their bodies.

When you contemplate a thought or action that is actually unhealthy, it triggers a subtle bad feeling in the body. Healthy feelings are usually soft, flowing, pleasant and energizing. Unhealthy feelings are usually hard, stiff, stuck and unpleasant.

So you may be facing a decision. You feel as sick as a dog but you have a message that a friend wants to visit you. What do you say? You consider the options. How would you feel if she came? And how would you feel if you said no?

You're unsure, so you do a little meditation. You bring her image to mind and notice how your body responds. If you feel it perking up in anticipation, you know that her visit will be healthy for you. If, however, the body sags and you feel a sense of gloom, you realize she wouldn't be good for your health.

We can think about issues relating to treatment for weeks and never get any clearer. The body, however, can tell you almost immediately. If you meditate, you are much more likely to "know in your bones" what is right for your body and soul.

Telling Yourself and Others

One issue you'll face may be, "Who do I tell?" Where do you find your personal point of balance between the extremes of panic and denial, between obsession and leading "an ordinary life"?

Do you even tell yourself you have cancer? Some part of you could be saying, "I'm not going to think about this. I'll do what the doctor says, but that is all!" It can take weeks or months or even years before the full significance of a serious cancer is absorbed by the psyche. It's your choice how quickly or slowly it sinks in.

If you take it in too slowly, you can just drive the feeling underground. You may pretend there is nothing to worry about, but some part of you knows you are lying. Even if the Grim Reaper knocks just once and walks away, that knock should wake you up.

For your own mental health, you need to absorb the full significance of a serious illness, sooner or later. If you try to downplay it or live with irrational hope, there will always be a deep tension within you, shutting out the part that knows the truth. That tension will equally derange your body's homeostatic balance. Finally, the best way to let the body do its healing work is to be at peace with the truth, even if that seems hard to do.

✸
Notes
✸

CHAPTER ONE

1. Elaine Marieb, R.N. Ph.D., *Essentials of Human Anatomy and Physiology*, Addison Wesley Longman, New York, 2000, p.9.
2. Robert Sapolsky, *Why Zebras Don't Get Ulcers*, W. H. Freeman and Co., New York, 1998, p.7.

CHAPTER TWO

1. Any good book on stress will describe the functioning of the autonomic nervous system. The information in this chapter comes mostly from books by Goleman, Sapolsky, Nuland and Pelletier listed in the bibliography.
2. Daniel Goleman, *Emotional Intelligence*, Bloomsbury, London, 1996, p.13.
3. Dr. Sherwin B. Nuland, *How We Die*, Chatto and Windus, London, 1994, p.69.
4. Daniel Goleman (ed.), *Mind Body Medicine*, "Hostility and the Heart," p.55.
5. Goleman (ed.), *Mind Body Medicine*, "The Relaxation Response," p.255–6.
6. Herbert Benson, M.D., and Miriam Klipper, *The Relaxation Response*, Avon, New York, 1976, p.87.
7. Benson, *The Relaxation Response*.

CHAPTER THREE

1. Goleman (ed.), *Mind Body Medicine*, "Hostility and the Heart," p.65.
2. Sapolsky, *Why Zebras Don't Get Ulcers*, p.42

3. Sapolsky, *Why Zebras Don't Get Ulcers,* p.42

4. Nuland, *How We Die,* p.69, and Sapolsky, *Why Zebras Don't Get Ulcers,* p.59.

5. Sapolsky, *Why Zebras Don't Get Ulcers,* p.159.

CHAPTER FIVE

1. Goleman, *Mind Body Medicine,* p.65

2. Sapolsky, *Why Zebras Don't Get Ulcers,* p.24

3. Goleman, *Mind Body Medicine,* p.26

4. Nuland, *How We Die,* p.69

5. Sapolsky, *Why Zebras Don't Get Ulcers,* p.159

6. Goleman, *Mind Body Medicine,* p.245

CHAPTER SIX

1. Nuland, *How We Die,* p.67.

CHAPTER SEVEN

1. Goleman, *Mind Body Medicine,* p.118

CHAPTER EIGHT

1. Goleman, *Mind Body Medicine,* "Asthma: Stress, Allergies and the Genes," p.196

CHAPTER TEN

1. Goleman, *Mind Body Medicine,* "Chronic Pain," p.113.

2. John Sarno, M.D., *The Mindbody Prescription,* Warner Books, New York, 1999, p.49.

3. Goleman, *Mind Body Medicine,* p.227.

4. Jon Kabat-Zinn, Ph.D., *Full Catastrophe Living,* Delta, New York, 1990, p.31.

CHAPTER ELEVEN

1. Thomas Leaman, M.D., *Healing the Anxiety Diseases,* Plenum Press, New York, 1992, p.28.

CHAPTER TWELVE

1. Dr. Hans Seyle, *The Stress of Life*, McGraw-Hill, New York, 1984, p.59.
2. Sapolsky, *Why Zebras Don't Get Ulcers*, p.77.
3. Leaman, *Healing the Anxiety Diseases*, p.86.

CHAPTER THIRTEEN

Most of the information in this chapter is derived from Pelletier, *Mind as Healer, Mind as Slayer*, and Sapolsky, *Why Zebras Don't Get Ulcers*.

1. Goleman, *Mind Body Medicine*, "Mind and Immunity," p.55.

CHAPTER FOURTEEN

1. Goleman, *Mind Body Medicine*, "Infertility, Pregnancy and the Emotions," p.213.
2. Robin Baker, *Sperm Wars*, Fourth Estate, London, 1996, p.118.
3. Sapolsky, *Why Zebras Don't Get Ulcers*, p.110.
4. Sapolsky, *Why Zebras Don't Get Ulcers*, p.113.
5. Sapolsky, *Why Zebras Don't Get Ulcers*, p.110.

CHAPTER FIFTEEN

1. Leaman, *Healing the Anxiety Diseases*, p.85–109.

CHAPTER SEVENTEEN

1. Herbert Benson, M.D., *Timeless Healing*, Fireside, New York, 1997, p.27.

CHAPTER TWENTY-TWO

1. Goleman, *Mind Body Medicine*, "Emotions and Cancer," p.89.

✺

Bibliography

✺

Baker, Robin, *Sperm Wars,* Fourth Estate, London, 1996. Entertaining and brilliant account of the way the mind affects sexual function.

Benson, Herbert, M.D., and Miriam Klipper, *The Relaxation Response,* Avon, New York, 1976. This perfect little book describes the physiology of stress and the effects of meditation. Benson, a highly respected researcher, has also written *Beyond the Relaxation Response* and *Timeless Healing.*

Goleman, Daniel, Ph.D. (ed.), *Mind Body Medicine,* Consumer Reports Books, Yonkers, New York, 1993. This book contains 25 articles by the most respected researchers in the field. Up-to-date, accurate and written for the lay audience.

Goleman, Daniel, Ph.D., *Emotional Intelligence,* Bloomsbury, London, 1996. An up-to-date analysis of the interaction of mind and feeling. Also see his other books, *The Meditative Mind* and *Vital Lies, Simple Truths.*

Kabat-Zinn, Jon, Ph.D., *Full Catastrophe Living,* Delta, New York, 1990. Describing the famous program of the Stress Reduction Clinic at the University of Massachusetts, using meditation and awareness with people suffering chronic pain and illness. Also see his book *Wherever You Go, There You Are.*

Kornfield, Jack, *A Path with Heart,* Bantam, London, 1993. This entertaining and authoritative instant classic by a leading Western meditation teacher and psychologist describes every aspect of the meditative process.

Leaman, Thomas, M.D., *Healing the Anxiety Diseases,* Plenum Press, New York, 1992. Linking stress to illness from a psychologist's perspective.

Nuland, Dr. Sherwin B., *How We Die,* Chatto and Windus, London, 1994. Entertaining bestseller describing the ways in which our bodies deteriorate.

Pelletier, Kenneth, Ph.D., M.D., *Mind as Healer, Mind as Slayer,* Delacorte, New York, 1992. This excellent, readable and scientifically rigorous analysis of the body/mind connection is a classic in its field. Also see his *Holistic Medicine: From Stress to Optimum Health.*

Rossi, Ernest, *The Psychobiology of Mind-Body Healing: New Concepts of Therapeutic Hypnosis,* Norton and Co., New York, 1993. Brilliant, technical, rigorous analysis.

Sapolsky, Robert, *Why Zebras Don't Get Ulcers: An Updated Guide to Stress, Stress-related Diseases and Coping.* W. H. Freeman and Co., New York, 1998. My favorite reference book! Entertainingly written by an eminent educator and supported by 75 pages of detailed references.

Sarno, John, M.D., *The Mindbody Prescription,* Warner Books, New York, 1999. Sarno cogently explains the role of the mind in causing and curing chronic pain.

Seyle, Hans, *The Stress of Life,* McGraw-Hill, New York, 1984. This revised edition summarizes the life work of the most renowned researcher in the field. Seyle combines high scientific standards with a willingness to explain his findings to the average well-educated person.

Index

Other Ulysses Press Mind/Body Titles

TEACH YOURSELF TO MEDITATE IN 10 SIMPLE LESSONS: DISCOVER
RELAXATION AND CLARITY OF MIND IN JUST MINUTES A DAY
Eric Harrison, $12.95
Guides the reader through ten easy-to-follow core meditations. Also
included are practical and enjoyable "spot meditations" that require
only a few minutes a day and can be incorporated into the busiest
of schedules.

HERBS THAT WORK:
THE SCIENTIFIC EVIDENCE OF THEIR HEALING POWERS
David Armstrong, $12.95
Unlike herb books relying on folklore or vague anecdotes, *Herbs
that Work* is the first consumer guide to rate herbal remedies based
on documented, state-of-the-art scientific research.

SIMPLY RELAX: AN ILLUSTRATED GUIDE
TO SLOWING DOWN AND ENJOYING LIFE
Dr. Sarah Brewer, $15.95
In a beautifully illustrated format, this book clearly presents physi-
cal and mental disciplines that show readers how to relax.

HOW TO MEDITATE: AN ILLUSTRATED GUIDE
TO CALMING THE MIND AND RELAXING THE BODY
Paul Roland, $16.95
Offers a friendly, illustrated approach to calming the mind and
raising consciousness through various techniques, including basic
meditation, visualization, body scanning for tension, affirmations
and mantras.

KNOW YOUR BODY: THE ATLAS OF ANATOMY
2nd edition, Introduction by Emmet B. Keeffe, M.D., $14.95
Provides a comprehensive, full-color guide to the human body.

THE JOSEPH H. PILATES METHOD AT HOME:
A BALANCE, SHAPE, STRENGTH & FITNESS PROGRAM
Eleanor McKenzie, $16.95
This handbook describes and details Pilates, a mental and physical
program that combines elements of yoga and classical dance.

PILATES WORKBOOK: ILLUSTRATED STEP-BY-STEP GUIDE
TO MATWORK TECHNIQUES
Michael King, $12.95
Illustrates the core matwork movements exactly as Joseph Pilates
intended them to be performed; readers learn each movement by
simply following the photographic sequences and explanatory
captions.

SENSES WIDE OPEN:
THE ART AND PRACTICE OF LIVING IN YOUR BODY
Johanna Putnoi, $14.95
Through simple, accessible exercises, this book shows how to be
at ease with yourself and experience genuine pleasure in your
physical connection to others and the world.

THE 7 HEALING CHAKRAS:
UNLOCKING YOUR BODY'S ENERGY CENTERS
Brenda Davies, $14.95
Explores the essence of chakras, vortices of energy that connect the
physical body with the spiritual.

101 SIMPLE WAYS TO MAKE YOUR HOME & FAMILY
SAFE IN A TOXIC WORLD
Beth Ann Petro Roybal, $9.95
Sheds light on common toxins found around the house and
offers parents straightforward ways to protect themselves and their
children.

WEEKEND HOME SPA: FOUR CREATIVE ESCAPES—
CLEANSING, ENERGIZING, RELAXING AND PAMPERING
Linda Bird, $16.95
Shows how to create that spa experience in your own home with
step-by-step mini workouts, stretching routines, meditations and
visualizations, as well as more challenging exercises to boost
mental potential.

*To order these books call 800-377-2542 or 510-601-8301, fax 510-601-8307,
e-mail ulysses@ulyssespress.com, or write to Ulysses Press, P.O. Box 3440,
Berkeley, CA 94703. All retail orders are shipped free of charge. California
residents must include sales tax. Allow two to three weeks for delivery.*

✺

About the Author

✺

Trained in the Buddhist traditions of Burma and Tibet, Eric Harrison has practiced meditation for more than 30 years. After one particularly intensive retreat, Harrison was encouraged by the monks to begin teaching meditation to others "in his own way." Over the years he has developed a method adapted to Western culture, one that eschews mysticism while emphasizing meditation's practical effects. As the director of Perth Meditation Centre, Harrison has worked closely with local doctors and patients to develop appropriate meditation programs for particular ailments. He lives in Perth, Australia.